AMERICA'S CENTENNIAL CELEBRATION

(Philadelphia—1876)

AMERICA'S CENTENNIAL CELEBRATION

CELEBRATION

(Philadelphia—1876)

by

Floyd & Marion Rinhart

A DELL

BICENTENNIAL

SPECIAL

(1st Edition)

LIBRARY OF CONGRESS CATALOGING IN PUBLICATION DATA:

Rinhart, Floyd.
  America's centennial celebration.

  Bibliography: p.

  1. Philadelphia. Centennial Exhibition, 1876.
I. Rinhart, Marion, joint author. II. Title.
(T825.C1R56 1976b) 607'.34'74811 75-38858
ISBN 0-914042-08-4

Published by Manta Books, P.O. Box 9445, Winter Haven, FL 33880

COVER by HALLINAN ADVERTISING AGENCY

This book manufactured in the United States of America.

ACKNOWLEDGEMENTS

We are deeply indebted to our son George R. Rinhart, Litchfield, Connecticut, who generously allowed us to photograph centennial views from his valuable collection of stereographs.

Our special thanks to George Moss, Jr., Rumson, New Jersey, who offered us warm hospitality and the use of his fine collection of New Jersey stereographs.

We would like to thank the staff of Rollins College Library, Winter Park, Florida, for their kind help during our research.

Our deep appreciation is expressed for the interest and encouragement given our project by Dr. Robert W. Wagner, Department of Photography and Cinema, Ohio State University, Columbus, Ohio.

TABLE OF CONTENTS

FOREWORD

The United States of America celebrated its 100th birthday with the opening of the Centennial Exposition on a sunny day, the 10th of May, 1876, and ending in a chill November rain of that year. Held in Philadelphia's West Fairmont Park, it was the first world's fair organized in the United States, and the biggest Fourth of July an American boy or girl ever had.

Photographs of the period add a particularly rich and interesting dimension to our national heritage. This book documents the problems and procedures involved in organizing the Centennial; the celebrations, both local and national, which took place; the opening and closing ceremonies; plus comments and dialogues which marked the end of our first hundred years.

The reader is taken on a verbal and visual tour of the major exhibits which displayed the nation's ingenuity, enterprise and culture in ways which astonished sophisticated visitors from abroad, gave rise to pardonable pride among the home folks, and inspired Edwin Godkin, editor of *THE NATION* to characterize Americans as "far less raw and provincial than their fathers; they have read more, they have mixed more with people of other nationalities, they have thought more and have had to think more, they have spent more for ideas and they have given away more."

It is significant that this national birthday party was conceived as an International Exposition. The inaugural event, the starting of the great Corliss steam engine which ran almost continuously for six months, was shared by the President of the United States and the Emperor of Brazil. In the Great Hall of Machinery, as recorded in the following pages, Bayard Taylor, a popular writer of the day reported: "North and South America started the machinery of the world." In his opening remarks, the President also emphasized the international importance of this uniquely national event:

"That we may the more thoroughly appreciate the excellencies and deficiencies of our achievements, and also give emphatic expression to our earnest desire to cultivate the friendship of our fellow members of this great family of nations, the enlightened agricultural, commercial and manufacturing people of the world have been invited to send hither corresponding specimens of their skill, to exhibit on equal terms, in friendly competition with our own. To this invitation they have generally responded. For so doing we render our hearty thanks."

In 1876 the art of photography was only 37 years old. The Centennial included the largest international photographic display since the great Crystal Palace Exhibition in London in 1851 and while the latter event was the highlight of the daguerrean era (with all three awards for excellence in daguerreotype going to Americans), photo-historian Robert Taft characterized the exposition in Philadelphia as "the high-water achievement of the American wet plate photographer."

Daguerreotypes were shown in the Centennial Exhibition, but the majority of the photographs were prints made from collodion negatives. William Henry Jackson sent 2′ x 3′ transparencies of scenic views of the American West while other U.S. photographers represented included: Sarony of New York; Brady of Washington; Carbut of Philadelphia; Bierstadt of Niagra Falls; Watkins of San Francisco; Bigelow of Detroit; Ryder of Cleveland; Landy of Cincinnati; and C. D. Mosher of Chicago.

The Photographic Art Building, an annex to the Gallery of Art, had 19,000 feet of exhibition space under a glass roof, and was built at a cost of $26,000 raised through subscriptions by the National Photographer's Association.

The Exposition was not only an occasion for the exhibition of photographs. It was also a massive picture-making event. The Centennial Photographic Company had the concession for official photography of the Exposition itself, including buildings, grounds, and exhibits. The company also had a gallery on the grounds where three camera operators, in a single day, reportedly made 873 portraits of visitors—by the wet plate process! Dozens of stereographs were produced as souvenirs of the Exposition, many of which the Rinharts have searched out and reproduced in the pages that follow. The strangely depopulated appearance of many of these views is accounted for by the fact that the wet plate required exposures of several minutes so that the only identifiable human figures are that at rest—sitting on benches or standing in static positions—while moving figures which thronged the streets and aisles appear as blurs, or "ghosts," or not at all.

C. D. Mosher, a Centennial award winner, and far-sighted photographer, produced a series of portraits titled, "Mosher's Memories of the Past," with the following legend printed on the reverse side of each:

> By special request, the negative from which this Cabinet Portrait is printed was taken for one of the series of Mosher's Historical Autograph Albums of prominent men and women. When completed the Albums are to be classified according to their profession and business of the person's photograph they contain, are to be deeded, with valuable statistics to Chicago, and preserved with the city archives, in memorial safe in the Court House, with special reference for their historical information. The safe is to be opened only once in every quarter of a century, from the fourth day of July, 1876, and then with appropriate and imposing ceremonies. The Offering, with its portraits and historical reminiscences, will be placed on

exhibition in Memorial Hall, at the second and third Centennial
anniversaries of our Republic. 'Tis then they will become rare re-
plics of the past (that we cannot now afford to lose the golden op-
portunity in giving), as it will be of great importance and value to
our descendants and the historian.
>   *"When other men our lands will till,*
>   *When other men our streets will fill,*
>   *And other birds will sing as gay—*
>   *As bright the sunshine as to day,*
>   *A hundred years from now."*

Awards also went to photographers from more than twenty other nations, including Julia Margaret Cameron and H. P. Robinson of England, and William Notman of Canada.

In 1876, we were a nation of 38 states and 46 million people, including immigrants coming in at a rate of 3.5 million for the decade ending in 1875. One-fifth of our population was then foreign-born and three-fourths of all Americans still lived on farms. Yet, the times were strangely like those of today, 100 years later, which precede our Bicentennial Celebration of the nation. Both events occur in periods of extremely rapid social and technological change, follow a divisive war, scandals in government, and a storm of passions which make logical decisions difficult, if not impossible. There was and is a need for healing; for looking to our heritage; for reflection and redirection; and for recapturing something of the American dream which we once shared. The Centennial events seem to accomplish that.

However, in 1876, who among even the most optimistic would have believed that before the next hundred years had passed Americans would be speaking to fellow Americans from the moon? How would the historically-minded Mosher react to the American scene if he could have been present at the opening of his Historical Autograph Album in 1976? Who knows what the state of the nation will be in 2076?

We can, however, with confidence and pleasure, look back and, through this Centennial book, this Family Album, experience something of the great celebration of our first hundred years and recapture some of its sights. Along with the recent experience of the Bicentennial, it may recall an old and useful lesson of history which is that we are what we are because we were what we were; and that while we can't escape our past we are continually adding to it through pictures, words, and deeds. The next hundred years is always in the making.

> *Robert W. Wagner*
> *Professor*
> *Director of Graduate Studies*
> *The Department of Photography and*
>   *Cinema*
> *The Ohio State University*

A Centennial Fair In the Making

**OLD LIBERTY BELL,
INDEPENDENCE HALL, 1876**

When Congress passed the immortal Declaration of Independence on July 4, 1776, the bell was the first to ring out the glad tidings about 2 p.m. on that joyous day. One hundred years later, the bell still remained the symbol of American liberty.

A CENTENNIAL FAIR IN THE MAKING

America was adrift in the late 1860's. The holocaust of war had disrupted the national purpose leaving the country far from united. Passion, not reason, prevailed and cool heads were in demand. Something was needed where all Americans could join hands in a testimonial to their common heritage—something that could and would unite a war-torn nation into a new and steady course.

A historic moment was at hand. In 1876, the *Declaration* of *Independence* would have its hundredth birthday—an event born in the shadow of candle and oil. The birth of the nation should be commemorated on a grand scale—a great healing celebration, a jubilee—where from all over the country proud Americans could come to celebrate the centennial and honor past sacred traditions.

Philadelphia had been the birthplace of the historic document—the guide to the country's greatness. Old buildings, relics of 1776, still stood within the city proper. The *"Cradle* of *Liberty,"* Independence Hall, had been carefully preserved as a shrine for the patriotic. With such a heritage, it was not surprising that a number of learned gentlemen, at an 1869 midsummer meeting of the *Franklin Institute,* should propose historic *Philadelphia* as the ideal background to show off the progress of the nation's one hundred years. The men proposed a world's fair—a collosal one—much larger than anything seen on the North American continent. A grand theme emerged from the thoughtful group—a great glittering exhibition to demonstrate to the European nations, the scope and magnitude of America's progress in the arts and manufactures—a splendid fair which would outshine the great *Paris Exposition* of 1867. Further, *Philadelphia* would become the hub of the centennial celebration.

For almost fifty years the *Franklin Institute* had been holding an annual science, art and manufacturer's fair in *Philadelphia.* These exhibitions had won national recognition, and its members were well-qualified to develop the idea of a world exhibition into a reality. The Institute's officers, adept at proper procedure, set the proposal into motion and a select committee of influential men, graphically named *The Centennial Commission* was formed to lay the plan before the *Philadelphia* city councils. This centennial commission had no direct connection with *Franklin Institute,* rather they were men of political bent. The proposal was presented before the city fathers with graceful expertise and with a vision of unparalleled prosperity and millions of visitors admiring their city, the city councils could not refuse. They enthusiastically gave life by voting money to the project. With this initial beginning, it was easy to persuade the state government to endorse the proposal with additional financial backing. The commission was now underway. However, if the envisioned world exhibition was to become the focal point for the 1876 celebration, it was imperative to have national recognition. To this end the *Centennial Commission* petitioned Washington for a charter.

National approval for the world's fair came when Congress passed a resolution on March 3, 1871, giving the commission about what it wanted—a formal acceptance of its work and the exclusive use of its official title—*"The Centennial Commission."* The bill provided that a delegate from each state be on the commission and that henceforth it would keep the President and Congress informed of its progress. However, it was a disappointment that the bill specifically excluded the use of federal funds for the venture.

The new permanent *Centennial Commission,* including state representatives, held its first meeting, in March, 1872, as guests of the City of *Philadelphia.* The commission wisely elected as its president the Honorable *Joseph R. Hawley* of Connecticut. General *Hawley,* of Civil War fame, was in the high council of the Republican party and a man of superb executive ability . . . just the right man to get things moving.

With patriotic zeal, the *Centennial Commission* settled down to work—spirit, force, and ardor became the mottoes of the day. Numerous subcommittees were appointed and began busying themselves with the long job ahead. The overall details of the fair were being molded and shaped.

Obtaining land for exhibition grounds was of first concern—about 200 to 300 acres. The site chosen was the unimproved acreage in sprawling *Fairmount Park,* ranging along the *Schuylkill River.* It had all of the components needed to make the exhibition successful—ready transportation, water, and a reasonably level terrain.

Dipping into the well of past experience, the commission made a detailed study of the *Paris Exposition* of 1867. Slowly a general pattern for the exhibition began to emerge: five main buildings with some 50 acres under roof, walks, landscapes, plus a generous portion of land to be alloted for other structures and displays.

Cost estimates began coming in, and it was soon found that ambition had far outstripped available financial resources. Again the *Centennial Commission* turned to Congress for formal help for another charter was needed . . . and finally approved on June 1, 1872. A *"Centennial Board of Finance"* was then empowered under the *Centennial Commission,* "to raise money upon the sale of stock and to attend to all duties necessary to bring the work of the exhibition to a successful issue." The board could secure subscriptions of capital stock not to exceed ten million dollars, and the price of each share was set at ten dollars. The charter specified that money raised would be used for the erection of buildings, fixtures, and other expenses necessary to complete the exhibition

**FRANKLIN INSTUTUTE EXHIBITION,
PHILADELPHIA, 1874**

For almost fifty years **Franklin Institute** *had held annual fairs which exhibited interesting items of science, arts, and manufactures. Back in 1869, several learned gentlemen of the Institute suggested that in view of the forthcoming centennial, an* **International Exhibition** *should be held. They also said that* **Philadelphia**-- *the birthplace of the nation--would be a most fitting site for the occasion.*

and, at the close of the fair, the assets would be converted to cash, and a pro rata settlement made to stockholders.

The remainder of 1872 found the Board of Finance the only hope for progress as the *Centennial Commission* had suspended the activities of other departments for lack of money. The success of the exhibition was threatened by the year's end for despite the issuance of circulars and public addresses to the people, response had been poor. Meanwhile, a seal had been adopted by the commission bearing the legend *"The United States Centennial Commission"* surmounting a vignette of *Independence Hall* with the prophetic sentence below—*"Proclaim Liberty throughout the land unto all inhabitants thereof."*

"In 1776 this building stood beyond the thickly settled portion of the city, and in what was known as 'The Fields.' A garden, enclosed by a brick wall, occupied the site of the house which now stands on the corner. The house was new, and the situation was so pleasant, that it at once attracted the attention of that dear lover of nature, **Thomas Jefferson,** *when he came to Philadelphia to take his seat in the Continental Congress. 'I rented the second floor,' he tells us, 'consisting of a parlor and bedroom, ready furnished.' He paid thirty-five shillings a week for his rooms, and in the parlor he wrote the Declaration of Independence upon a little writing-desk three inches high, which still exists."*

Early in 1873 the period of quietude had passed. The work of the innumerable money-raising committees and subcommittees was now beginning to show tangible results. Patriotic citizens attended a great mass meeting on Washington's birthday—which turned out to be a very successful day for the sale of stock. Committees made up of trade and professional groups sold shares to their fellow workers.

The *Centennial Board of Finance* had auspiced a *"Woman's Centennial Committee of Pennsylvania"* which turned out to be a great army of willing workers and fund raisers of top ability. By the spring of 1873, a little over three million dollars had been raised . . . approximately half coming from patriotic citizens and the balance from the *State of Pennsylvania* and the *City of Philadelphia.*

With money in hand, the exhibition now had a substantial and firm business footing. *John Welsh,* one of *Philadelphia*'s most successful merchants, was elected by the stockholders to be president of the *Centennial Board of Finance. Welsh* had headed the *Sanitary Fair Commission* during the Civil war and was an experienced and proficient leader. The cloud of financial uncertainty had been cleared, the crisis passed.

The *United States Centennial Commission* went to work with renewed vigor and confidence. Architects were called in and invited to submit sketches and designs. Surely the time was at hand for national coverage of things to come, complete with oratory, and what better day than the *Fourth of July* for the event to be held in *Fairmount Park.* A handsomely decorated stand was erected on the site of the proposed *Memorial Building.* The honored speakers, as they looked out over the still barren landscape, envisioned the great exhibition to come. They spoke of the hallowed ground on which they stood and how it was steeped in Revolutionary War history. On the grounds had been the site of the old *Peters* homestead, *Belmont. Richard Peters* had been one of the stalwarts of the 1776 era, a secretary to the Continental Congress, and one of the first patriots to suspect *Benedict Arnold* might not have been all that met the eye. *George Washington,* sacred now in the memory of Americans, had been a frequent visitor to *Belmont,* and one French visitor had called Belmont "a tasty little box in the most charming spot nature could embellish." A Proclamation from *President Grant* ended the ceremonies, announcing to the world, "An international exhibition would be held in the city of *Philadelphia* in 1876."

A whirlwind of ideas for the fair was being tossed about, but many were unsound. Meanwhile, in the same spring of 1873, a large and elaborate world exposition opened in Vienna with about seventy thousand exhibitors. An exploratory visit to the *Vienna Exposition* would seem a partial solution to finding out many practical details for layouts and structural designs for proposed buildings. A local engineering firm, *Wilson* and *Pettit,* had been engaged by the centennial organization as consultants, and young *Henry Pettit* volunteered to go to Vienna without pay—traveling expenses his only compensation. *Pettit* brought back ideas very helpful to the building and arrangement committees, and his on-site inspection brought alterations to a number of plans

**CONCOURSE AT BELMONT,
FAIRMOUNT PARK, C. 1872**

*The still barren landscape of **Belmont** as it must have
appeared to the speakers at the Fouth of July event in
1873 at Fairmount Park. The oratory gave national
coverage about the great exhibition to come.*

under consideration. An important finding was that the huge main exhibit building in Vienna was inadequate for display purposes because of its circular shape.

In response to competitive architect awards, a number of designs for the principal buildings were submitted to the *Centennial Commission* in the Fall of 1873. The building committee was far from satisfied—some designs were too expensive, others presented a fire hazard. Many questions as yet remained unanswered. Should the structures be of steel or wood? Should windows be used or skylights? The problems of dismantling after the close of the exhibit had to be considered. The working out of the thousand details was more complicated than the building committee had anticipated.

A great financial panic was sweeping over the nation in Autumn of 1873 and unfortunately it was late in the year when the building committee approved an elaborate plan for the main building. The finance committee promptly rejected it as being too costly. More architects were called in and other plans were considered and debated. Slowly the building costs were reduced but never, it seemed, low enough to gain the finance committee's approval. The building board, in near desperation, turned to *Wilson & Pettit* for deliverance, in the Spring of 1874. A tentative plan for the main building, in size and shape, had been approved by the board, but its cost was still the big factor, and a twenty percent reduction was needed for the cost target was $100,000 per acre of floor space. Mr. *Pettit* came up with an ingenious solution where others had failed—he redesigned the roof and shifted the aisle areas and finally the building, finance and executive comittees joined hands.

The finance committee had, meanwhile, petitioned Congress, in April, for money to help with the projected additional costs. Congress failed to pass the bill.

About this same time, Spring of 1874, Washington discovered to its dismay that it had been remiss concerning the international aspect of the exhibition. In the original centennial charter, no one in the United States Government, even to the presidency, had been empowered to officially invite foreign nations or exhibitors to participate. Fortunately, the matter was cleared with the passage of a bill on June 5th of that year.

Adequate bridge construction to take care of the heavy traffic ahead—workers, construction materials, goods, and people—was going forward at a fast pace. A new bridge was being built across the *Schuylkill River* at *Girard Avenue*. The hundred-foot-wide structure was being acclaimed . . . "the widest bridge in the world." Also, a handsome wrought iron *South Street* bridge was under construction at the same time.

Other forthcoming marvels were being rumored in the Spring of 1874—the most exciting one being the *Phenix Iron Company* was to build a centennial observation tower of iron 1,000 feet high! However, the rumor was unfounded.

The time for oratory was over by the Summer of 1874. An agreement was signed with a *Philadelphia* contractor, the low bidder, and work commenced immediately—an encouraging sight to the now uneasy centennial organization.

With the *Main Building* scheduled at a deadline date of January 1, 1876, *Pettit & Wilson* focused their energies on designing the *Machinery Building*, the second largest projected structure to be built on the fairgrounds . . . some fourteen acres under one roof.

The *Centennial Commission*'s burden was financially lightened considerably in the summer of 1874 when both the *State of Pennsylvania* ($1,000,000) and the *City of Philadelphia* ($200,000) agreed to supply funds for two of the five main buildings. The two buildings in question, *Memorial Hall* and *Horticultural Hall*, were designated to become permanent museum-type buildings which would remain on the grounds after the fair closed. Both contracts were awarded before the end of the year and construction on *Memorial Hall* soon underway.

The year 1875 heralded the shape of things to come. The welcome sounds of hammer, saw, and rivet pervaded the air when the great army of workmen descended on the fairgrounds. Reaction to the government's invitation to foreign exhibitors was prompt and overwhelming. Requests for land and display space poured in. The application from Great Britain and its far-flung Empire, alone, was staggering—innumerable under-roof spaces and building lots on the grounds for three large buildings to house their administrative staff. Any doubts about the exhibition having an international flavor were put to rest—Spain, Sweden, Brazil, Japan, and others requested building lots for structures which would reflect their cultures.

IRON SPRING, FAIRMOUNT PARK, C. 1870

VIEW FROM FAIRMOUNT PARK, C. 1870

Only a few years before the Centennial Exhibition, the area adjoining Fairmount Park *had been under-developed land with stretches of grassland, wooded ravines, and forest. On the Schuylkill River, a number of small steamboats plied between the famous Water Works at* Fairmount *and the* Falls *of* Schuylkill. *Row boats could be hired on the river above the dam at* Fairmount.

The government in Washington may have been slow in providing financial aid for the grand exposition, but it was not reluctant to display its virtues as a working government by erecting its own buildings on the exhibition grounds. A special appropriation provided "that from the Executive departments . . . there should appear such articles and materials as would, when presented in a collective exhibition, illustrate the functions and administrative faculties of the Government in time of peace and its resources as a war power, and thereby serve to demonstrate the nature of our institutions, and their adaptations to the wants of the people." A board, approved by *President Grant,* representing the seven major bureaus of the government, quickly went into action and soon an 85,800 square foot building, in the shape of a Latin cross, was underway. The Smithsonian and Interior departments would have about one half of this area for their displays, the balance to be divided among the other five departments. Two small buildings, to stand adjacent to the government's main building, were also authorized.

Meanwhile, requests for parcels of land had come in from a number of states desiring space for the building of edifices which would reflect their back-home architecture and show off their native wares and products.

Early in the winter of 1875, the important *Pettit-Wilson* designed *Machinery Hall* was placed under contract and work started. Of the commission's five main buildings, only *Agricultural Hall* remained unsettled. An outside architect was called in, his plan accepted and, finally, in June, work on the last of the big buildings was underway. The cost of the three buildings, to be paid for by the *Centennial Commission,* was estimated to be $2,200,000. Expenditure for walks, streets, comfort stations, water supply, operating and other miscellaneous expense was still to be accounted for. Up to that date, some $1,800,000 had been raised from private subscription and a mortgage seemed unavoidable by the summer of 1875. A final effort to obtain money from Congress was made.

Ever since 1873, the *Women's Centennial Committee* had worked like the proverbial beaver to raise money for the exhibition. Their endeavors had spread to thirty-six subcommittees—one in each state. Stock-selling fetes had been held in music halls, opera houses, ballrooms, and parks. The women had given luncheons, clambakes, and tea parties in the style of *Martha Washington.* A fund-raising sale of special commemorative teacups and saucers as momentoes had been one of the highlights in their clever bag of tricks. A distinctive committee, led by the indefatigable Mrs. *E. D. Gillespie,* of *Philadelphia,* gripped the lapels of politicians and lobbied in Washington. By 1875, prestige and praise had been their reward—"America should be proud of her women. From the days of the Revolution until now they have always come nobly forward . . . and their work for the Centennial is their crowning glory . . . full credit should be awarded for their patriotism."

Now the good ladies wanted something for themselves—a woman's pavilion at the centennial fair where the skills and products of a woman's hand could be exhibited. Again, *Mrs. Gillespie* and her many friends went to work. Donations

**VIEW FROM GEORGE'S HILL OF THE EXHIBITION
GROUNDS UNDER CONSTRUCTION**

From right to left, beyond the cedar fence, are
Massachusetts State building, Connecticut State
building, New Hampshire State building. *To the left,
the vacant lot is the site of the future* State building of
Michigan. *The large building beyond [shaped like a
cross] is the* United States Government Building.

WALK NEAR ENTRANCE TO FAIRMOUNT PARK, C. 1875

Fairmount Park *made a charming place for a day's outing. Its fine water views, facilities for boating, and other natural attractions had no equal in America according to a tourist guide of 1873.*

PARIS EXPOSITION, JULY 1, 1867, DISTRIBUTION OF AWARDS

A vast and brilliant throng gathered at the **Palace of Industry** *to watch the* *emperor himself bestow the awards. The American exhibitors did well--3* *grand prizes, 17 gold, 66 silver and 94 bronze medals.*

Dapper and young, **Henry Pettit,** *Philadelphia* *civil engineer and consultant to the* **Centennial** **Commission,** *played an important part in the* *overall planing of the* **Centennial Exhibition.** *Many of his suggestions and ideas were put* *into operation and it was his design for the* **Main Building,** *which saved the day when cost* *factors had brought the exhibition to a virtual* *standstill.*

began pouring in from the states—*Florida* the first with $47.50, *Massachusetts* for $5,000, *Rhode Island* for $4,000, $1,000 each from the cities of *Trenton* and *Camden*—the list went on until more than $30,000 had been raised. By midsummer of 1875 work on the structure was begun.

With construction speeding ahead and the many smooth-working committees handling the details of their departments, the *Centennial Commission* turned to the matter of awards, prizes, and citations. The commission reviewed the Paris and Vienna expositions for guidance and protocol. Republican America wanted none of the pretentious show put on by the French Emperor in 1867. The French had made their awards from a stage hung in royal velvet, covered with gold bees and surmounted by a gigantic imperial crown. Long strips of green and gold had hung from the glass roof. The garish show had awarded ten ornate trophies, 64 grand prizes, 883 gold medals, and 3,653 silver medals. The commission decided Americanism would be their guide, simplicity their theme—bronze medals, struck by the mint, and classical diplomas would be conferred. A general classification for awards was arranged:

1. Mining
2. Manufactures
3. Education and Science
4. Art
5. Machinery
6. Agriculture
7. Horticulture

To award the honors, a committee of some two hundred impartial judges were appointed, equally divided between Americans and foreigners; each judge an expert in his particular sphere of knowledge. A special building for the judges was recommended with office and operating space.

The talents of *Wilson* and *Pettit* were kept busy in the first half of 1875. After finishing the design of *Machinery Hall,* they went to work on the hundreds of problems which hung like untidy strings, awaiting settlement. First, the undertook the beautification of the grounds and many walks. Next, they designed and placed two bridges, north of *Memorial Hall,* over the *Lansdowne* and *Belmont* ravines, thus creating a place where nature lovers or tired fair-goers could rest shielded from the hustle and bustle of the exposition. Seven miles of attractive walkways were laid out. A three-acre artificial lake was scooped out and dressed about its borders with garden shrubbery, vases, and fountains. To supply water for the exposition, a pumping station with an output of a million gallons a day was built on the west bank of the *Schuylkill River.* Some three miles of cedar fencing, nine foot high, was needed to enclose the gigantic 236 acres of fairground. Facaded and pretentious comfort stations and concessions for cold drinks and snacks had to be located here and there for convenience. The *Centennial Commission* found certain types of competitive exhibits ill-suited to be held with the fairground proper, and so twenty-two acres located about four hundred yards outside the main entrance, was acquired for the exhibition of livestock. This area contained 1,500 cattle stalls and other outbuild-

HORTICULTURAL HALL, INTERIOR

"The liberal appropriations of the City of Philadelphia have provided the Horticultural Department of the Exhibition with an extremely ornate and commodious building, which is to remain in permanence as an ornament of Fairmount Park." The architect was H.J. Schwarzmann who also designed Memorial Hall, the only other permanent structure on the exposition grounds.

TUFTS ARCTIC SODA WATER, 1876

Billed as the largest in the world, Tufts $30,000 refreshment stand was next to the popular Globe Hotel *outside the fair grounds. The 40 foot high fountain of variegated marble glittered with silver trimmings. Fashionable* Elm Street *strollers could quench their thirst from 76 syrup, 8 soda or 20 mineral tubes.* James Tufts *also had soda water concessions inside the exhibition grounds.*

ings for storing hay, straw, and grains. Bedding and feed were supplied by the commission at cost prices, whereas the stalls were free to exhibitors. The entire outside space resembled a typical large American country fair for other lands were also procured outside the grounds—one for testing of mowing and hay-making machines, and another for testing tillage and plowing implements.

By the early Fall of 1875, progress at the centennial grounds was like a wondrous tale from the Arabian Nights. Thousands of curious visitors viewed the astonishing scene. January 1, 1876 had been the deadline for many of the buildings, but the fair was fast taking shape. The *Main Exhibit Building* was well ahead of schedule—its vast expanse of glass had been glazed, the tin roof put on, the inside floor laid, and painting underway. Because of its monstrous size, it was almost impossible for visitors to comprehend that four hundred men were still working on the building. Over two hundred workers pushed *Machinery Hall* to its October completion date. The granite walls of *Memorial Hall* were in place, and the large dome nearly ready. *Horticultural Hall* stood finished except for plastering and many of the other buildings, scattered over the broad expanse of the fairgrounds, were in various and active stages of construction, reflecting the toil of three thousand workmen. The panoramic scene resembled a swarming beehive.

Outside, but near the exhibition grounds, on *Belmont Avenue,* the stark wooden frame of the 1,150 room *Globe Hotel,* stood outlined against the sky as sheathing and roofing were being applied. While at the intersection of *Belmont* and *Elm,* work was in progress on the *Trans-Continental Hotel* which would have 500 rooms. Both hotels, when completed, would appeal to the affluent fair visitor at $5.00 per day—*Philadelphia*'s highest. The nearby *Atlas Hotel,* with its 1,300 rooms and capacity for 5,000, would be less expensive—from a dollar a day and upward. All in all, by the time the fair opened, more than 2,000 hotels and regular boarding houses would be in readiness for the huge influx of visitors. Also, a visitor's service called "*The Centennial Lodging House Agency*" would meet the travelers' trains and guide them to comfortable and moderately priced lodgings.

Congress, in its 1875-76 session, after years of refusing financial aid to the centennial exhibition, reversed itself and granted a loan of $1,500,000. With the loan was a stipulation that when the fair closed, the government would be repaid first, before the stockholders, from the assets. On February 16, 1876, *President Grant,* giving the ceremony an old-time flavor, signed the bill into law with a quill from the wing of an American eagle shot near *Mount Hope, Oregon.* The continuous search for more money was over!

Diary

of

Centennial Notes

January 1 - May 10

INDEPENDENCE HALL.
PHILADELPHIA, 1876

Philadelphia held a great event at **Independence Hall** *to ring in the Centennial year. As one reported, "Gaslights of pyramidal form were exhibited in each window of the lower floor of the hall, and the doorway had a row of lights on each side. The balcony above was brilliant with Chinese lanterns, and the upper windows were bright with candles. The national colors were hung wherever it was possible to place them, and in all the variety and beauty that flags, streamers, jacks, and banners could impart. The coats-of-arms of the thirteen original States occupied a conspicuous position, and over the main entrance was a medallion twelve feet in diameter, encircled with evergreens. It represented Washington at the altar of liberty, with the genius of America, and was of tasteful design. A large shield and the flags of all nations further embellished the building, and Greek fires, Roman candles, and calcium lights made the scene one of great brilliancy."*

CENTENNIAL CELEBRATIONS

January 1—The opening of the year 1876 was celebrated with great rejoicing throughout the country. The people thronged the streets at midnight, illuminated the hill-tops with bonfires, and gave a universal welcome. In *Philadelphia,* the great event was held at *Independence Hall.* At midnight, as the bell in the old tower tolled the knell of a dying year, the new flag, made for the occasion, was hoisted to the flagstaff in front of *Independence Hall,* and flung to the breeze. The Second Regiment of the National Guard, drawn up in line for the purpose, fired a salute of 100 guns, and the patriotic emotions that had been stirred up in thousands of hearts found vent in deafening cheers. The flag is the exact counterpart of the one unfurled by Washington on January 1, 1776, at Charlestown, Massachusetts.

The Commissioner of City Property had made extensive arrangements for the illumination of the hall and its surroundings. Other buildings in the vicinity were illuminated, the *Philadelphia Press Clubhouse,* and all along *Chestnut Street,* stores, clubhouses, offices and hotels were ablaze with light.

The old chime bells at *Christ Church* where *General Washington* worshipped rang a hallelujah peal at midnight. *St. Stephens* and *St. Peter*'s chimes were additions to the melody.

At *Hartford, Connecticut,* the year was ushered in by the ringing of bells and the firing of a salute of thirty-eight guns, one for each State and one for Colorado, by the order of the mayor. At midnight the fire-alarm bells struck 1-7-7-6, and at half-past twelve 1-8-7-6.

Norwich and *New Britain, Connecticut,* also celebrated by bell-ringing and bonfires.

In New York, the year was inaugurated at midnight by the ringing of bells, setting off fireworks, and the screaming of steamboat and locomotive whistles. Great crowds were in the streets and Broadway was packed with people, including ladies, as if at midday. The bells of the fire department sounded the numbers 1-7-7-6 and 1-8-7-6, and the *Trinity Church* chimes rang many patriotic airs.

At Washington, the Methodist churches held meetings watching the old year out and the new year in. Just before twelve o'clock all the fire-alarm bells were sounded and struck 1-7-7-6, and at exactly midnight struck 1-8-7-6. The engines, with full head of steam, were run into the street and their whistles blown at midnight. The War Department furnished the necessary ammunition, and loaned a cannon to the District Commissioner, who at midnight caused a salute of 37 guns to be fired. The *Metropolitan Church* chimes rang out the advent of the new year.

"THE CRADLE OF LIBERTY."
1876

At *Portsmouth, New Hampshire, Captain Leo Marvin,* of the *Portsmouth Artillery,* aroused the sleeping citizens by greeting the Centennial year with a salute of 38 guns from two brass twelve-pounder pieces, captured by *Sir William Pepperell* at the battle of *Louisburg.* The salute was fired at the south part of the city, on land owned by *Hon. John Elwyn,* and which descended to him from his ancestors, who acquired it from the Indians in the early days of the settlement of the State. This artillery company was raised by the order of the *Provincial Congress,* June 5, 1775, and has been in existence ever since. Under joint direction of the company and a committee of the board of trade the event was appropriately honored, the following programme having been decided upon: suspension of business in the afternoon; ringing of bells one hour at sunrise, noon, and sunset; firing of salutes in the evening. The city government and fire department met at City Hall, and were escorted by the *Portsmouth Artillery* and marine band to the temple, where a mass centennial meeting was held, *Mayor Goodrich* presiding. Patriotic music, instrumental and vocal, was interspersed.

In *Worcester, Massachusetts,* the occasion was observed in a most enthusiastic manner, and the hills surrounding the city were crowded with huge bonfires. A salute of 100 guns was fired, and numerous private displays of fireworks were made.

At *Springfield, Massachusetts,* the new year was greeted with lights, bells, whistles, and firing of guns at the United States armory.

At *New Haven, Connecticut,* a meeting under the auspices of *Admiral Foote Post,* G.A.R., was held. At midnight a flag was raised on the city green, and a salute of thirteen guns fired. Then the fire-bells rang 1-8-7-6 five times, and a huge bonfire was lighted at the corner of Church and Chapel streets.

At *Altoona, Pennsylvania,* there was a grand demonstration, consisting of a midnight parade of the Fire Department and different societies, a general illumination and a meeting in the Opera House.

At *Lockport, New York,* the event was ushered in by a midnight torchlight procession of firemen, music, firing of cannon, ringing of bells, and bonfires.

The parade at *Poughkeepsie, New York* was a magnificent and successful affair. The national colors were displayed at all points from both public and private buildings, and the air was rent with shouts and cheers for nearly an hour.

Similar celebrations were observed at *Newport, Woonsocket,* and *Pawtucket, Rhode Island;* and at *Mobile, Alabama,* the *Mystic Society* made a brilliant display.—*Record of the Year.*

**VIRGINIA CENTENNIAL VIEWS.
TOBACCO EXCHANGE, RICHMOND.**

**VIRGINIA CENTENNIAL VIEWS.
WASHINGTON'S HEADQUARTERS,
RICHMOND.**

January 1—At the Centennial buildings at *Philadelphia*, two workmen were killed outright, and another died from his injuries.—*Record of the Year.*

January 4—The *State Archaeological Society* at *Columbus, Ohio*, resolved to attempt to form auxiliary societies in each county of the State, and take steps to have the society fully represented at the Centennial by a full collection of relics, models, and plans relating to the prehistoric period in Ohio, which is rich in such matters.—*Record of the Year.*

January 6—The ladies of *Lowell, Massachusetts*, assisted by the ladies of adjoining towns, gave a tea party at *Huntington Hall*, to obtain funds in aid of the *Centennial Exhibition* at *Philadelphia*. A notable feature of the occasion was the sale of tea cups and saucers used at the refreshment tables. These were decorated from original designs drawn by the ladies of *Lowell*, intended to be commemorative of the centennial year.—*Record of the Year.*

January 9—A very rich deposit of gold was struck in the Centennial lode, near *Laramie City, West Texas*

January 23—The year 1876 is remarkable in other particulars besides that it includes the Centennial fourth of July. It is a leap year. It contains fifty-three Sundays, which the clergymen must remember. It contains fifty-three Saturdays, which the employers of weekly labor, payable the last day of the week, must remember.—*Boston Daily Advertiser.*

January 24—The Secretary of the Treasury of the United States addressed the following letter to the Secretary of the Interior: Sir: I have the honor to inform you that it has been represented to this department that the regulation requiring an oath to an invoice of goods intended for the International Exhibition, to be taken by the owner, manufacturer, or duly authorized agent of such owner or manufacturer, and verified by a Commissioner, United States Consul, or Consular Agent, will occasion inconvenience and expense, and may properly be dispensed with. Should such goods be withdrawn from the exhibition for sale or consumption in the United States, an invoice sworn to as heretofore prescribed will be necessary.—*Record of the Year.*

January 25—The Centennial appropriation bill passed the national House of Representatives by a vote of 140 to 130.—*Record of the Year.*

February 2—A severe gale swept over many portions of the United States. At *Philadelphia* the towers of the Centennial buildings were severely damaged.—*Record of the Year.*

PLANTING THE CENTENNIAL TREE, HIGHLAND PAARK HOTEL GROUNDS, AIKEN, SOUTH CAROLINA, APRIL 15, 1876.

February 9—The *Centennial Appropriation* was debated in the Senate.—*Record of the Year.*

February 11—Senate passed the *House Centennial Bill,* appropriating $1,500,000, by a vote of 41 to 15, without amendment.—*Record of the Year.*

February 21—The President of the United States deemed by Executive Order the twenty-second day of the present month a national holiday and that all business in the Executive Department of the government be suspended on the 22nd of February, 1876, and departments closed on that day.—*Record of the Year.*

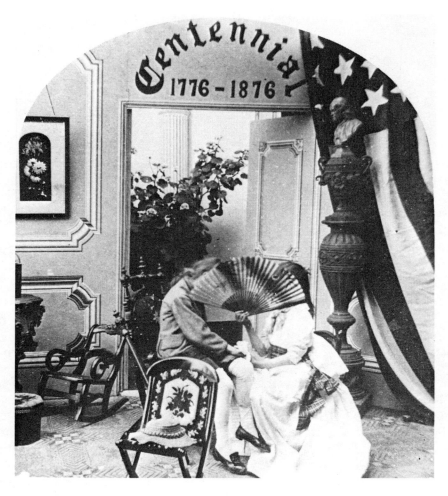

As the year 1876 approached, a spirit of national pride was abroad the land. After a century of trial and conflict, it was a time for reflection--a time, also, to reminisce about colonial days and deeds of the nation's forefathers. The year would breathe nostalgia and patriotism; it would be a healing year when the birth of the nation would be commemorated on a grand scale.

February 22—Washington's birthday was very generally observed as a holiday throughout the United States. In New York business was suspended, and there were parades and festivities. At *Richmond, Virginia,* there was a celebration, consisting of a vice-regal court-ball of the time of *Lord Botetourt,* and in *Philadelphia* the day was even more generally celebrated. *Martha Washington* receptions and Centennial tea-parties were held in the afternoon and evening in various localities.—*Record of the Year.*

February 29—House. Certain officers were instructed to restore the writing on the *Declaration of Independence.*—*Record of the Year.*

March 1—An important bill was passed by the house, March 1, recommending the people of the several States to assemble in their respective counties or towns on the approaching Centennial anniversary, and to cause to be delivered a historical sketch of the county or town from its formation, copies of which are to be filed in the County Clerk's office and in the *Library of Congress,* so that a complete record may thus be had of the progress of the republic.—*Harper's Monthly Magazine.*

March 2—The question of classification of the enormous number of objects to be exhibited at our World's Fair next May is one that has been most satisfactorily settled by giving it up entirely. The result of the present classification will be manufactures for the main hall, machinery for the *Machine Hall,* etc. In plain terms, there will be no classifications whatever besides the natural one indicated by the buildings. Spain is arranging her exhibit. Spain has 11,253 square feet facing on the nave between Egypt and Russia. A grand picture of Columbus and his Spaniards discovering America will be displayed.—*New York Times.*

March 3—*The Centennial Plaza.* From the corner of *Elm Street* and *Belmont Avenue,* the visitor looks northward across the Grand Plaza which lies between the *Main Exhibition Building* and *Machinery Hall.* The Plaza is nearly 500 feet wide, and here the railroad tracks focus. Workmen are at present engaged in removing the debris and arranging walks and plats.

The *Judges' Pavilion, Photographic, United States, Woman's* and many other buildings occupy the middle ground, while in the distance may be seen the *Southern Restaurant,* the unfinished *Agriculture Building,* and the picturesque structure erected by the *State of New Jersey.* It has lately been determined to add to the *Art Building,* the *Main Exhibition Building,* and some others, the new work made necessary by an unexpected pressure for space. Many of the prominent metropolitan journals will erect buildings for the use of their representatives and friends. Workmen have been busy during almost the entire winter in laying up sod, arranging the beds, and planting shrubbery.—*Harper's Weekly.*

**CENTENNIAL ARCH,
CHARLESTOWN BASE, MASS.**

Centennial decorations commemorating the victorious action on Bunker Hill, June 17, 1775.

**CENTENNIAL CELEBRATION IN
CAMBRIDGE, MASSACHUSETTS.
MANSION OF ZACHARIAH BORDMAN.**

The citizens of historic Massachusetts, began commemorating local Centennial events in 1875, which in no way lessened their enthusiasm for celebrating the nations's one hundredth year with parades, meetings, and other festivities.

44

THE 5TH MARYLAND REGIMENT, PARADE GROUNDS, JUNE 17TH, 1875, BATTLE OF BUNKER HILL.

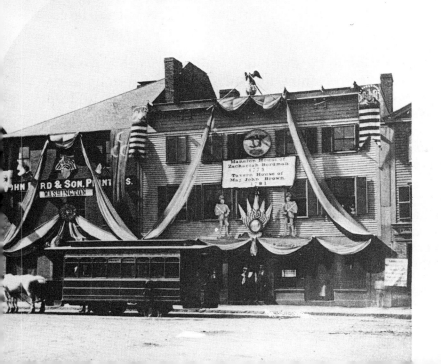

March 3—*Richmond, Virginia*—A resolution was introduced in the Senate today to allow certain parties to have the use of the original will of *George Washington,* now among the records of *Fairfax Courthouse,* for the purpose of having it photolithographed for the preservation of the facsimile and for use at the Centennial Exhibition. A bond of $10,000 is to be required for its safe return.—*New York Times.*

March 4—Things at *Philadelphia* are beginning to foreshadow the great coming event, and this in the unpleasant rather than the agreeable sense. Hotel keepers reluctant to let rooms to single men, the obvious reason married couples occupy same amount of space. The prices have not yet advanced. But with boarding-houses, a specialty of enterprise conducted by females, prices have gone up fifty per cent. Many do not intend to take permanent boarders but reserve their rooms for transient guests and to add more beds to rooms. The boarding-house districts expect to rely on the overflow from hotels. While the boarding-house keepers are preparing to transmute the overflow from the hotels into a golden shower, there are various schemes in different stages of development for utilizing the inevitable indignation of the public with the boarding-house keepers. There is a *Granger Company* which proposes to erect wooden barracks in a park not far from the Centennial ground, which will accomodate 3,000, and their charge will be fifty cents per head. The whole thing will be conducted after the fashion of a camp-meeting.—*New York Times.*

March 5—A grand concert will be given under the auspices of the *Woman's Centennial Union,* at *Steinway Hall, New York* on next Saturday evening. Instrumental music will be provided under the direction of Mr. *Theodore Thomas,* and some principal soloists of the City have been engaged for the occasion. On the following Saturday an operatic matinee will be held at the *Academy of Music.* These entertainments merit public support, their success will add largely to the *Woman's Centennial Fund.*—*New York Times.*

March 5—The price of admission to the exhibition will be fifty cents, payable in one note. The receivers at the recording turnstiles will have nothing to do with the notes, except to decide whether they are good or bad, and to drop them in the boxes.—*New York Times.*

March 6—*London*—*Admiral Worden* publishes a notice that the United States steamer *Franklin* will receive goods at *Southampton* for the Centennial Exhibition until the 13 inst.—*New York Times.*

March 7—A circular has been issued by the ladies of the *Central Centennial State Committee* at *Albany* asking the women of the State to unite with them in sending a State banner to the *Women's Hall* at *Philadelphia* and assist in raising an endowment fund for *Mount Vernon.*—*New York Times.*

March 7—Mrs. *Gillespie,* President of the *Women's Department of The International Exhibition,* will be in *New York* on March 9, having been invited by the *Women's Centennial Union* to address the women of New York. The meeting will take place at *Chickering Hall* at 2 p.m. All are cordially invited to attend.—*New York Times.*

March 9—Signs of promise everywhere at the Centennial. The decoration of the *Main Building* completed. Near the main entrance some of the nations are as busy as bees. The Spanish enclosure is already up, and from the hints of decoration, will be exceedingly rich, both in carving and gilding. One vessel loaded with things for the Centennial has already arrived at Havana.—*New York Times.*

March 9—A meeting of the *New York Centennial Union* was held in *Chickering Hall,* at which Mrs. *Gillespie,* of *Philadelphia,* explained the women's centennial movement and the present condition of affairs. About 500 ladies were present. Mrs. *Cullum,* who is the granddaughter of *Alexander Hamilton,* introduced Mrs. *Gillespie* as the granddaughter of *Benjamin Franklin.* Mrs. *Gillespie* said she was not the granddaughter of *Franklin,* for that would make her ninety-two years old, which she certainly was not. Mrs. *Gillespie* said all inventions of women would be exhibited if useful in any way, but nothing that was merely fashion of ultra kind would be exhibited. Mrs. *Whitney* asked what the country had done for women that the women should do so much for the country. The applause was great when Mrs. *Gillespie* replied, "It has made us the freest women in the world . . ."—*New York Times.*

March 9—The *Treasurer* of the *Centennial Board* of *Finance* acknowledged the receipt of $500,000, being the first installment of the appropriation by Congress in aid of the Exhibition.—*Record of the Year.*

March 10—An ode written by *Sidney Lanier* of *Georgia,* entitled *"The Centennial Meditation of Columbia"* to be sung at the opening ceremonies of the *Philadelphia Exhibition,* May 10, 1876.—*Record of the Year.*

March 14—Austria at the Centennial. Mr. *Alfred Buek,* the *Secretary* of the *Austrian Commission* to the *Centennial,* has arrived in *New York,* and will leave for *Philadelphia* on Thursday next. The goods which are to be placed upon exhibition were shipped in the steamship *Hammonia* which left Hamburg on Saturday last, direct for *Philadelphia.* There will be over 500 exhibitors. The space alloted in the main building covers an area of 24,000 square feet and will adjoin the German and Russian exhibits. One feature is a large collection of oil and water color paintings for the art annex.—*New York Times.*

GRANGER'S HOTEL,
PHILADELPHIA, 1876

"The Grangers may have hayseed in their locks, but they certainly have brains under their hair." The **Pennsylvania Grangers,** *an organization of farmers, resisted the idea of high transportation and boarding-house costs to the* **Centennial Exhibition.** *They were determined to provide accomodations for themselves and for their brother Grangers from other States. First of all they made friends with the railroads [their avowed enemies].* The **Pennsylvania Central** *gave to them the use of a great tract of land at* **Elm Station,** *about four and a half miles from the* **Main Exhibition Building.** *Further, the railroad contracted to make a charge of 15 cents round trip to the fair. Contracts were then let for the erection of wooden sheds to accomodate 2,400 people for a camp-meeting style residence. The prices proposed were 50 cents for lodging and 50 cents for each meal.*

March 15—Regular meetings of the *New York State Centennial Board* and of the *Advisory* and *Selection Committees* on *Works* of *Art* were held at the *International Exhibition* offices. The *Dairymen's Association* of the State asked for an appropriation to make a creditable exhibition at the Centennial. Complaints received by board of applicants to the Centennial not being notified about space allotments. While *New York State* will be represented in all departments, the art department will be especially fine and attractive, excelling that of any other state. The works to be exhibited include productions of deceased and living American artists and works of foreign artists owned by Americans.—*New York Times.*

March 16—The arrival of the Spanish engineers was quite an event for the *Philadelphians,* who welcomed the Iberian soldiery most heartily. *Prince Oscar* of *Sweden* to attend exposition.—*New York Times.*

March 17—Mr. *Perrault,* the *Secretary* of the *Centennial Commission,* has today received a telegram announcing the arrival at *Montreal* of sixty large packages of goods for the *Centennial Exhibition.* The first train of fifteen cars will leave *Montreal* on Tuesday next for *Philadelphia,* loaded with goods and all the castings and other fittings for the Canadian department of the Exhibition.—*New York Times.*

March 20—The cards of invitation for the *Centennial Exhibition* have been designed by *Dreka* of *Philadelphia,* who rivals *Tiffany* of *New York* in this particular, and are now being engraved. They are rather large doubled sheets similar to those used in fashionable society. At the top is a shield shaped something like a shell, and on each side is the legend, 1776-1876. On the shield is the inscription, *"The Centennial Year* of the *United States of America."*—*New York Times.*

March 23—We are surrounded on every side with evidence that this is the centennial year. We put on our centennial boots and wear our centennial necktie, eat from dishes of centennial ware and read the centennial papers. We smoke centennial cigars, lighted with centennial matches. We look at our centennial calendar for the day of the month, and find out when the sun rises by consulting our centennial almanac. We receive centennial communications written on centennial paper, with centennial pens dipped in centennial ink. We attend centennial tea parties, purchase centennial relics and admire ladies dressed in centennial robes. Before this centennial year is departed we shall all learn how noble a thing it is to suffer and be strong.— *Millville* (New Jersey) *Republican.*

March 24—The *Argentine Republic* and *Chile* are neighbors also in the allotments of space in the *Main Exhibition Hall.* Thrity thousand articles to arrive from the *Argentine Republic.* The department of Chile, her pavilion, her pyramidal trophy, and her fourteen upright ornamental double-faced cases are all prepared, and are now receiving the final touches of the decorator.—*New York Times.*

March 25—The steamship *Hammonia* will arrive in *Philadelphia* tomorrow and has on board all the goods from *Switzerland* intended for the *Centennial Exhibition.*

March 29—House.—The bill providing for the expenses of admission of foreign goods to the *Centennial Exhibition* was passed.

March 29—Several gentlemen belonging to the *Mexican Centennial Commission* arrived in New York on the steamship *City of Merida,* from *Vera Cruz,* via *Havana.* The gentlemen brought with them 228 cases of goods for the exhibition, and expect a second load will arrive by the next steamer. Among the articles are a number of objects of art from the *Academy* of *Fine Arts* of the *City of Mexico,* principally paintings. Also there will be a collection of minerals. Of manufactured articles there are fabrics, cigars, filagree silverwork, and porcelain. Also a collection of works of celebrated writers of the country on science and education. A large number of national and Indian costumes will make an interesting feature of the exhibition.—*New York Times.*

March 29—The award of a premium of $1,000 for the best bale of cotton offered by the *Memphis Cotton Exchange,* for exhibition at the *Philadelphia Centennial,* was made today to *William Taylor,* of *Lee County, Arkansas.*—*New York Times.*

April 3—A Centennial land claim. Attempt of a *North Carolinian* to secure the lands around the exposition buildings—an affair which created considerable stir in *Philadelphia.* A well informed lawyer of *Philadelphia* said the land claimed was seventy miles up the *Delaware River,* near *Stroudsburg.*—*New York Times.*

April 7—The different railroads interested in the subject of Centennial fares have met in convention, and have settled that there shall be a reduction of twenty-five per cent, and that round trip tickets shall be issued for a period of sixty days. The *Union Pacific* does not consent to this arrangement.—*New York Times.*

April 7—*Halifax.*—The crew which is to compete in the Centennial regatta at Philadelphia have commenced training. *New York Times.*

AUDITORIUM. OCEAN GROVE, NEW JERSEY

The famous auditorium was decorated with a grand display of flags for the Centennial and in readiness for its summer camp meeting activities. A parade was planned for the Fourth of July, to be concluded with a reading of the Declaration *of* Independence.

CENTENNIAL PIER, CAPE MAY, NEW JERSEY

Congress Hall Pier [*above*] *was renamed to suit popular fancy during the Centennial year.* **Cape May,** *within easy reach of* **Philadelphia,** *was visited by tired Centennial sightseers who enjoyed the cooling breezes and a dip in the Atlantic.*

April 7—A meeting of the *Boston Light Infantry* was held tonight to perfect arrangements for attending the *Fort Moultrie Centennial*, at *Charleston, South Carolina.—New York Times.*

April 8—Mr. *Jopling, British Superintendent* in the section of fine arts of the *United States Centennial Exhibition*, sailed yesterday from *London* and is bringing 56 water color drawings, many engravings and architectural designs, 197 oil paintings, of which more than 100 have been exhibited at the *Royal Academy*. Goods from France and Germany on way to the *Philadelphia Exhibition* by steamer.—*New York Times.*

April 14—Twenty-one carloads of goods were discharged at *Machinery Hall* this morning for exhibitions in that department. The steamship *St. Laurent,* from *Havre,* brought 500 cases of French exhibits.—*New York Times.*

April 19—House.—Mr. *O'Brien (Maryland)* introduced a bill for the coinage of Centennial silver dollars and half-dollars.—*Record of the Year.*

April 19—Local Centennial celebrations were held today at *Concord, Lexington, Salem,* and *Newton, Massachusetts.* The two latter cities kept the one hundredth anniversary of local events by brilliant social festivities. In *Salem,* a Centennial ball was given in *Mechanics' Hall,* under the auspices of the *Ladies' Centennial Committee,* and a large and fashionable assemblage was present, including Governor *Rice* and staff. At *Newton,* the children carried out with great success a *Martha Washington* reception. The historic towns of *Concord* and *Lexington* kept alive the famous 19th of April by observances which were carried out without any ostentatious display. At *Lexington* there was a so-called "antique and horrible" parade in the morning, with a grand military and civic ball in the evening. *Concord,* besides a parade of the artillery company in the morning, held a public meeting in the evening, followed by a ball.—*Record of the Year.*

April 20—About a thousand ladies gathered last evening in the great hall of the *Cooper Union,* in response to an invitation issued by the *New York Women's Centennial Union* to the business women of the City, to attend a Centennial meeting. Mrs. *Gillespie,* of *Philadelphia,* addressed the meeting.—*New York Times.*

May 1—The work of arranging for the opening of the exhibition is pushed forward with all possible activity and despite an enterprise on so grand a scale there is a good prospect that the 10th of May will find the buildings and grounds in satisfactory condition. The principal delays are in handling of goods because of the immense number constantly arriving. There is another cause of delay. Our own citizens have been remiss in their work and now at the eleventh hour rushing in their contributions to the display. The French and English far ahead of ours in preparation. Even the Australians have beaten our own exhibitors in point of time.—*Harper's Weekly*.

May 7—All eyes turned in direction of *Philadelphia. Fairmount Park,* with its glittering palaces of the industrial arts; with its throng of smaller structures, graceful and interesting; with its *Memorial Hall,* and its beautiful palm house, with its lawns, its parterres, bright with hyacinths and gaudy tulips, and its magnificent trees, its esplanades, its ravines, its bridges, its miles of asphalt pavement, its lakes, its fountains, its myriad things of interest and beauty—*Fairmount Park* is the topic of every tongue, and the subject of every contemplative mind.

Arrived in *Philadelphia,* the next point is to get to the *Centennial Grounds.* Assuming that the bulk of *New Yorkers* will be stationed at the *Continental* and other hotels along *Chestnut* and neighboring streets, there are for them the two-horse car lines of *Walnut Street* and *Market Street,* each of which is one block from *Chestnut.* Besides these there will be innumerable carriages at the command of the hotel proprietors, though it is feared that the prices will be high. There will be also the Centennial wagonettes, the fare of which will be fifty cents, and there will be some monstrosities of stages to hold fifty persons, drawn by ten horses, at twenty-five cents. The horse-car fare in *Philadelphia* is seven cents. One can take the steamcars from the depot on *Broad Street,* or the depot on *Green Street.* Besides this method, there is the steamboat line, which starts from the *Schuylkill River* at the foot of *Green Street.* This will convey passengers to a wharf at the foot of *Landsdowne Terrace,* on the top of which is *Horticultural Hall.* Boats will run every nine minutes, beginning at 7:30 a.m., 15 cents round trip. Visitors having carriages of their own should have the driver take them round by *Girard Avenue Bridge,* because this route is the approach to the eastern entrance to the grounds. Here the carriage can drive right up to the doors of the eastern end of the *Main Building,* and the visitors can step out of their vehicles into the building itself.—*New York Times.*

May 8—Great progress has been made since Saturday in the preparations for the opening of the *Centennial Exhibition.* Portions of *Memorial Hall* are ready, but there still remains a large quantity of scaffolding and material in the centre of the building. Many cars of the narrow-gauge railway are on the track and the managers promise to have them operating tomorrow.

At the larger hotels quarters have been engaged from Wednesday for many of the Governors of the States, with their suites, and representatives from foreign governments and other dignitaries.

In consequence of the pressure for seats, the dimensions of the grand platform, for the opening ceremonies on Wednesday, have been extended so as to accommodate 200 persons additional. The space reserved for the press has been enlarged so as to provide for 550 seats and fifty desks, and is located on

INSIDE MACHINERY HALL

Work supplies and display items were brought inside the fairgrounds with utmost efficiency. The **Pennsylvania Railroad** *laid about 3½ miles of tracks within the Exhibition grounds. These lines connected directly with the wharves on the Delaware and with all the railroads from distant points in the country, thus eliminating the transfer of goods from one freight car to another.*

**MAIN BUILDING, NAVE, LOOKING WEST,
BEFORE OPENING DAY**

*"Exhibitors must provide, at their own cost, all show
cases, shelving counters, fittings, etc. which they may
require...Exhibitors, or their agents, shall be
responsible for receiving, unpacking, and arrangement
of objects, as well as for their removal at the close of the
Exhibition."* From the **Director-General's Regulations.**

the flagstone plateau, near the grand orchestra.

The special point of attraction today was the site of the *Catholic Temperance Fountain,* the magnificent architectural adornment of the western section of the grounds where the formality of a public trial of the fountain's capacity was witnessed by a large assembly of invited guests. The completed fountain will be unveiled with ceremonies on July 4.—*New York Times.*

May 8—The through line of railroad from *Boston, Massachusetts,* to *Philadelphia,* without change of cars, was inaugurated.—*Record of the Year.*

May 8—The old *Franklin Press,* from the *Patent Office, Washington,* was received in *Machinery Hall* on Saturday. The police force will consist of 1,000 men. There will also be a competent detective force.—*New York Times.*

May 8—Boston.—Governor *Rice,* accompanied by Lieutenant Governor *Knight,* Secretary of State *Pierce,* and fifteen members of the Governor's staff, with the *First Corps Cadets,* 125 men, rank and file, as escort, left for *Philadelphia* tonight by the *Fall River Line. Brown's Brigade Band,* thirty pieces, accompanied the cadets. The *National Lancers,* 110 men, with the *Chelsea Band,* eighteen pieces, left by the *Stonington Line,* and will meet the Governor and party at *Jersey City* tomorrow morning and accompany them to *Philadelphia.* The entire party numbers 310.—*New York Times.*

May 8—The time for starting the special trains tomorrow, which are to take the Congressional guests to the opening ceremonies at the *Centennial Exposition,* have been again changed and the original programme adopted. The first train will leave Washington at noon, and the second at 3 o'clock.—*New York Times.*

May 9—The present aspect of the *Centennial Exhibition* grounds is most dispiriting, for the rain has fallen with a steady persistence all of last night and all day. It is true that among the various exhibitors many are quite ready, but there are others who are working like bees, and still will not be ready when the morrow comes. In and about the buildings the work of decoration and preparation has been going on all day, and will be continued throughout the night. "If only the sun will shine," is the burden of their song tonight.—*New York Times.*

May 9—President *Grant,* accompanied by his Cabinet and Mrs. *Grant,* arrived in *Philadelphia* this morning. The President and his wife went to the house of Mr. *Childs.* Shortly afterward the Congressional delegation reached the city. The Maryland delegation, comprising Governor *Carroll* and his staff, arrived here today, and put up at the *Girard House.* The *Maryland Centennial State Board* arrived at the same time, and Mr. *Childs* has invited the whole delegation to meet the President and Cabinet at his reception tomorrow evening. Governor *Rice* of Massachusetts, and staff, and military escort, arrived here

THE PENNSYLVANIA CENTRAL RAILROAD DEPOT, NEAR MAIN ENTRANCE TO EXHIBITION GROUNDS.

today, and were received by a battalion of the *First Regiment, City Troop,* who escorted the party to the *Continental Hotel.* The *Boston Cadets* then marched to the *Masonic Hall Hotel,* in *Chestnut Street,* where they will remain while in the city. Governor *Dingley* of *Maine,* and staff, are also in the city.—*New York Times.*

May 9—The staff of the *House* of *Tiffany* are here at the Exhibition, and have just placed in position, outside of their place, the life-size bronzes of the Nubian flambeau-bearers. Mr. *Moore,* the silver man of the house, is arranging a collection of testimonial goods which they have manufactured during the past twenty-five years, and have just announced that they have not space enough to show all their goods. The *Gorham Manufacturing Company,* next to them, are equally busy, and they will also make a fine exhibit. *Starr & Marcus* are wailing over their smashed cases, but will display fine cameos and jewels in some handsome small round cases that have survived the jarring of the railroad train and the energy of the baggage men.

Of foreign nations Japan is the busiest, and within the past few days has worked a complete transformation in the front part of her exhibition by the production of an immense number of superb bronzes. It is impossible now to give any idea of the charming appearance of the Japanese department, but it will assuredly be recognized as one of the best arranged and most interesting displays of the entire building.—*New York Times.*

May 9—The gigantic hotels near the grounds are comparatively free from anything like a crush this evening, but the hotels which cluster in the neighborhood of the *Continental,* the great hotel centre of *Philadelphia,* are simply jammed. The focus of all is the *Continental,* and its wide halls present the appearance of a covered street or arcade, through which a varied and surging mass of people are moving in a never ceasing struggle. There are men from all parts of this continent, and of others. The East and West have equally contributed its masses. Side by side with the pale-featured men of the busy East one sees Southerners from *Louisiana* and *Alabama;* bronzed and powerfully built men, whom it is easy to recognize are ranchmen, stock-owners, and miners, from the Western frontiers; men from *Maine,* who have come with the Governor of that State, and men from *California,* brought eastward by the Centennial. There are Englishmen, scores of them, who mostly look a little bored or bewildered by the dense crowd they find themselves part of. There are Frenchmen, Italians, Spaniards, and Germans. You can take your stand at one of the pillars in the hall, and in the course of fifteen minutes hear words spoken in nearly every language of Europe.—*New York Times.*

STREET-PASSENGER   RAILWAY   CONCOURSE,
NEAR   THE   MAIL   BUILDING,   EXHIBITION
GROUNDS.

INFORMATION FOR THE RAILROAD TRAVELER

PAY NO FEES TO EMPLOYEES—BUY TICKETS BEFORE GETTING IN THE CARS.

Safety rules:

Keep to your seat in case of accident.

Do not put head or arms out of window.

Avoid standing on platform while train is in motion.

Train conductors will assign passengers to their seats.

Smoking Cars are attached to all trains.

Handsomely fitted-up Drawing-Room and Sleeping Cars are attached to all trains. Reserved seats or berths on these cars can be obtained for an additional charge from any ticket office or car conductor. In these cars it is customary to pay a fee to the Porter of the car.

Travelers having through tickets and desiring to stop off can obtain lay-over checks.

Travelers should understand their tickets are good only for the railroad and route stamped on the ticket. Through cars should be inquired for.

The average speed on American Railways is between 25 and 35 miles per hour, including stops.

Accident Insurance Policies can be obtained at any of the principal Railway Stations for 25 cents per thousand dollars insured.

One Hundred Pounds of Baggage is allowed each regular fare railroad passenger. Overweight charges are at the rate of 15 percent of the passenger fare per 100 pounds. The traveler should be sure he receives a numbered metal check for each piece of baggage. In event of loss or damage, the railroads limit of responsibility is $100.00 for each package checked.

Excursion Tickets are good only as stipulated on the ticket.

Railroad trains make about a twenty minute scheduled stop at meal times, and the cost is almost a uniformly 75 cents per meal. Abundant notice is given before the train starts. Hand baggage left on the seat secures the seat for the owner.

Travelers approaching Philadelphia by rail can have their baggage delivered to any of the Hotels, Boarding Houses, or Residences by an agent of a transfer company who will pass through the cars. Generally a 50 to 60 cent delivery charge, for each piece, will be made.

From *Visitor's Guide*

An ever-increasing horde of travelers came to Philadelphia for the May 10th opening day festivities of the World's Fair *at* Fairmount Park.

HOW TO REACH THE CENTENNIAL GROUNDS.

The various horse railroads in the City or Philadelphia afford an amount of traveling accommodations not enjoyed by any other city in the world. The

PHILADELPHIA CITY PASSENGER RAILWAY
Via Chestnut & Walnut Street,

looking forward to the large business of 1876 have made special arrangements for the comfort of citizens and visitors. The total length of track used by this line is seventeen miles, including the two branches, one to Darby and one to the Park, this latter having its depot adjoining the Centennial Grounds, and landing the Passengers directly in front of the Main Exhibition Building and Machinery Hall. The Cars are nearly new, admirably finished, large and comfortable. Total carrying capacity 60,000 passengers per diem, using 108 cars, and employing 300 men and 1029 horses. These cars run on minute and minute and a half time. The new depot on Belmont Avenue is a model for comfort and convenience.

The Cars of this line pass the following places : University of Pennsylvania, West Chester R. R. Depot, Colonnade Hotel, Academy of Natural Sciences, New Public Buildings, U. S. Mint, Concert Hall, Chestnut St. Theatre, Fox's American Theatre, Continental and Girard Hotels, Washington House, Guy's Hotel, Independence Hall and Square, American Hotel, Custom House and Post Office, and within half a square of Philadelphia and Mercantile Libraries, Academy of Music and Horticultural Hall. First car leaves depot at Centennial Grounds at 4.30 A. M., last car leaves at 11.28 P. M.

CONTINENTAL HOTEL.

The most perfect Hotel in all its appointments in the United States. Accommodations for *1000* Guests.

J. E. KINGSLEY & CO., Proprietors,
PHILADELPHIA, PA.

Advertisement from **The United States International Exhibition,** *1875.*

PICTURES OF THE
CENTENNIAL BUILDINGS.

One of the most efficient means of awakening interest in the Centennial, has undoubtedly been the admirable series of pictures published by Mr. Thomas Hunter of this city. Starting with the "Art Gallery," the more wide-awake of our citizens eagerly seized upon it, and distributing it in large quantities to their friends and customers, the enthusiasm in our great national celebration steadily widened and deepened. Mr. Hunter has since added successively the other buildings and calls especial attention to the following list :

1. ART GALLERY,
2. MAIN BUILDING,
3. HORTICULTURAL HALL,
4. MACHINERY HALL,
5. AGRICULTURAL HALL.
6. Double, (Nos. 1 and 2 on a sheet.)
7. Triple, (Nos. 1, 2 and 3 on a sheet.)
8. Quintuple, (Nos. 1, 2, 3, 4 and 5 on a sheet.)
9. BIRD'S-EYE VIEW OF THE PARK, Buildings in the foreground.

All these pictures are of uniform style and price. The drawings were made under the immediate supervision of the respective architects, and have all the latest modifications in size and detail that have been found necessary. They are beautifully printed in three colors, on heavy plate paper, and not only convey a correct idea of what is being done for the great celebration, but will form a valuable souvenir when that event is over.

These Pictures are approved by the Centennial Board of Finance who have distributed these Pictures in large quantities in every civilized country.

Price 50 Cents each, sent free by mail, securely packed.

Prices in quantities are as follows :

Per Dozen, $4.00,   Per Hundred, $30.00,   Per Four Hundred, $100.00,
Per Thousand, $200.00,

Sent C.O.D. by Express or on Money-order. If sent by Mail, 40 cents per dozen extra for postage. No charge for printing card on one hundred and upwards. Tubes for mailing, in any quantities, 3 cents each. Agents wanted in every town, to whom liberal terms will be offered. The various agents for the Centennial Board of Finance are especially invited to act as agents for these pictures.

THOMAS HUNTER,
Commercial, Chromo and Photo-Lithographer,
716 FILBERT STREET, Philada., Pa.

Advertisement from **The United States International Exhibition,** *1875.*

ENTRANCE TO ROTUNDA

On the most conspicuous spot in the rotunda was placed the **Apotheosis of Washington,** *by the Italian sculptor* **P. Guarnerio. William Dean Howells** *wrote: "Washington perched on an eagle much too small for him. The group is in plaster; the eagle life-size and the Washington some six feet high from the middle up; having no occasion for legs in the attitude chosen, Washington thriftily dispenses with them. The poor man who made this thing is so besotted with it as to have placarded his other works, 'By the sculptor of Washington'."* **Edward Strahan** *wrote: "The Americans, by the bye, did not appreciate the statue of their chieftain, because the lower part of the bust was finished off with a gigantic eagle. The more ignorant ones surmised that it must be 'Washington on a Lark!'" As a work of portraiture, "We cannot refuse the sculptor very high praise...one of the best idealizations of the cast taken by Houdon that sculpture has ever furnished...and shows Washington as the peacemaker, in which the warrior is merged."*

Opening Day

Celebration

The veil of clouds lifted, the sun came out and all doubts of a dismal opening day were dispelled. A great orchestra, led by **Theodore Thomas,** *was located over the north entrance of the main building. The huge crowd was thrilled by renditions of national airs from various countries. The stirring music was followed by a prayer, after which a chorus of 1,000 voices sang* **Whittier's** *beautiful hymn. The applause was deafening. After a speech by* **Joh Welsh,** *the* **President** *of the* **Centennial Board** *of* **Finance,** *the choir sang a cantata composed by* **Sidney Lanier,** *of* **Georgia.** *Formal presentation speeches were then given, including one by President* **Grant.** *At the close of the President's address, a signal was given and "flags were hoisted to the buildings, the steam whistle sounded, guns boomed, and the grand inaugural of America's hundredth-year celebration was complete."*

BAYARD TAYLOR

From a daguerreotype. [Courtesy of Miss Josephine Cobb.]

TAYLOR, (James) BAYARD. (1825-1878).

In his time a well-known author, journalist, and later U. S. Minister to Germany. Popular as an author of travel narratives and best remembered for his English translation of Goethe's *Faust.* He wrote for the *Saturday Evening Post,* the *United States Gazette,* and the *New York Tribune* from which the following account is taken.

THE CENTENNIAL FAIR

The Exhibition opened with the
grandest ceremony ever witnessed in America

A REVIEW OF THE DAY
(A picture of the opening ceremonies
description by Bayard Taylor)

Philadelphia, May 10.—The American people may justly congratulate themselves. Energy, and a power of sturdy endurance rarely so tested before, have
atoned for all manner of indifference, negligence and accidental hinderance;
the elements, threatening until the last moment, became gloriously benign and
radiant; a hundred thousand people met under the dappled dome of the May-
day sky, and with prayer, grand orchestral music, and still grander choral song,
brief and fitting official formalities, and the closing jubilation of bells, cannon,
instruments, and voices, the *International Exhibition of* 1876, was opened. It
was a superb, a wonderful success. No such spectacle has ever before been witnessed in this country—probably none grander in all the essentials of expres-
sive show anywhere in the world. This auspiciously begins the commemoration of the Centennial year.

THE MORNING

Never were the aspects of a day so earnestly scanned. The crowds of last
night, as they gathered in the corridors of hotels, under awnings, and in the
abundant places of refreshment near the grounds, talked of little else than the
weather. It rained dismally, and the wind almost took on the rawness of a
northeast storm. But at the *Trans-Continental* (which was filled to its utmost
capacity) I met Probabilities, just arrived from Washington. To my daring
question: "What will be the weather tomorrow?" he answered in the calmest
tone: "Possibly cloudy—certainly no rain." With that oracle I made two members of the *Centennial Commission* happy.

VIEWS FROM THE PLATFORM

There is no great public spectacle in my memory with which I can compare it. The parallel lines of the two halls framed the picture on the north and south; but to the east and west, over a few detached buildings, there was only a fringe of pale green treetops against the sky. All this space, nearly half a mile in length by at least 250 yards in breadth, seemed to be filled with people. The greatest crowd within view at any time could not have been much less than 100,000 persons.

It was already evident that the thoughtless eagerness of the masses to get nearer the central point of interest would lead to trouble, if not to danger. The space reserved for the Press, immediately under the speaker's platform, was invaded by hundreds who broke through the lines, and reporting soon became anything but a pleasant occupation. It seemed quite impossible to restrain the tremendous impulse of the crowd. Gen. *Hawley,* prominent by his strong, manly face, a little pale from the weight of responsibility resting on him, gave a few quiet orders, the effect soon being visible. It seemed as if the efforts of a single line of policemen to stay the surging mass and the slowly stretching rope would be like Mrs. *Partington*'s attempt to mop up the Atlantic Ocean; but they worked manfully, and altogether, and the avenue for guests became clear again. The unhappy spectators in front could not really help themselves; each man was the head of a line, a thousand men deep, resting upon him. And had they not sincerely respected the authority which restrained them, they might have instantly swept away the representatives of the law; it was like a strong horse submitting to the will of a child. When the first backward push was made there were screams of terror and suffering, and presently a man in a dead faint was handed over the rope. Fortunately, there was no more serious accident, and I saw no signs of riotous resistance in that part of the crowd.

The appearance of such a mass of humanity was something remarkable. It took on a strange, enormous individuality, now seemingly agitated by a general tremulous motion, now writhing and undulating like the muscles under the scaly skin of a dragon. Out of the vast dark sea of heads arose the two granite pedestals, upon each of which some 30 or 40 persons had climbed, and there were daring boys on the bronze backs of the horses, clinging to their stumpy wings, or perched on the heads of the Muses. One, who came near sliding off the bevel of the base (from which he would have dropped upon the crowded heads below), and regained his place by a feat of strength, was rewarded by hearty applause. The sun burned upon all with a sultry fire which denoted more rain in store; but every cloud brought a cool and grateful breeze from the West.

INSIDE THE GROUNDS

At 9 o'clock, when the gates were opened to the public, the inward flow began, but it was some time before it kept pace with the increasing flow from without. The invited guests were first admitted half an hour earlier at the southern entrance of the *Main Building;* but when I reached that point only a few moments afterward, I found such a crowd of dignitaries with their ladies, chorus-singers, musicians and officials connected in some way with the Exhibition, that both time and endurance were required to pass the gate. Only one door of the building was opened, and hundreds of gentlemen and ladies surged and perspired for some time under the portal before they could reach the shadowy quiet of the interior. From the opposite portal, on the northern side, our way passed under the great platform erected for the orchestra and chorus—a cool dark passage, out of which we emerged into a bath of sunshine, and a vision of startling, almost stunning character. An innumerable crowd on either hand, kept back by ropes and lines of policemen, which swayed out until they nearly touched in the centre, and blocked our passage; the two Pegasuses, their ugliness hidden under masses of climbing and clinging humanity; the rising platform and whole front of the *Memorial Hall* equally heaped and crowded, the 900 singers and 200 musicians getting into place in the rear; lines of men clear against the sky, on every roof and pinnacle—these were the first prominent features of the view. Reaching the platform at last, where Mr. *Dixey,* the *Master* of *Ceremonies,* and a score of official aids, set the thronging guests to order, I found the best possible situation for studying the scene more in detail.

The early morn was overcast, and the blithe music of the chimes floated far over the land in the damp air. But the veil slowly lifted; the wind came out of the west, and specks of clear blue began to brighten and broaden. By 8 o'clock the transformation was complete; the leaden canopy of the past two days receded into a soft pearl-gray background of air, against which the sun-touched banners sparkled like tongues of flame. There was no longer a doubt of the day. People were already arriving from all points of the compass; in fact, they seemed to spring out of the ground in every variety of ready-made costume. Every street car was bursting with its load; country vehicles, decorated wagons, and private carriages thronged *Belmont Avenue* and that of the Republic at an early hour. Governors of States, officers of the army and navy, foreign and native exhibitors, happy guests with tickets and contented guests with silver half-dollars in their pockets, gentlemen, scholars, bummers, and adventurers jostled each other in whatever direction one looked. When I compared the street-pictures with those offered by Vienna, on that raw and chilly May morning of 1873, I knew that the scene to come would surely make me proud and satisfied as an American.

ARRIVAL OF GUESTS

All this while there was a constant stream of invited guests from the *Main Building*, through the narrow lane between the two great masses of people, and up the steps of the platform. They must have numbered in all hardly less than 4000, and a company at once so distinguished and so picturesque has never before been seen in this country. They came with an irregularity which was far more quaint than any intentional contrast could have been—Spanish and French officers, Japanese in cocked hats, Congressmen and Senators in full dress and the most nonchalant reverse diplomatic uniforms, Egytians, Norse, Chinese, ladies with lifted parasols, soldiers, and even broad-brimmed Quakers. Many famous persons passed undiscovered, but the people were sharp-eyed, and never failed to give notice of everyone whom they detected. Gen. *Sherman* was one of the first to be popularly hailed; then, after a few politicians, Gen. *Hancock* succeeded to the greeting. A little after ten the Emperor and Empress of Brazil—the latter in morning costume of pale blue silk—came out from under the musicians' gallery. *Dom Pedro*'s fine, intelligent, frank face and towering stature were at once recognized, and he was heartily cheered along the way. He lifted his hat and bowed repeatedly, with a bright, friendly smile, as if he felt the existence of a hearty good-will among the people.

Not long afterward a gentleman with a grayish beard had nearly reached the steps, when someone called out, "*Blaine!*" and then followed a burst of cheers. Secretary *Bristow* was not recognized until after the ceremonies were over, when the call of his name brought an equal response. On the right a man with a dusky face became conspicuous for his efforts to penetrate the crowd, and the air of combined strength and dignity with which he resisted its jostling. The policeman helped him over the ropes, somebody said, "*Fred Douglass!*" and he was loudly greeted as he mounted the platform.

There was a temporary interruption in the arrivals, caused by the irresistible rush of the crowd on the right, between the *Main Hall* and the bronze horses. The policemen lost their ground; a company of *Boston Cadets* was sent to their aid, and for a few minutes there was a scene of great confusion. The cadets charged gallantly into the very heart of the crowd; bayonets glittered, blue-and-white uniforms became scattered among the dark civilians, and the brave young fellows seemed to be getting the worst of it for a little while. A detachment of cavalry soldiers went to their aid, and a company of armed seamen from the Congress formed a wall on the opposite side. After that there was peace until the close. I could not learn that anyone was injured, beyond the usual pommeling in such cases, but it is a marvel that there were not many deaths from pressure and heat.

THE CEREMONIES

At a quarter past ten *Theodore Thomas* turned his back upon us, lifted his arms and brought down the first crash of music. The eighteen national airs, however, only reached us in fragments—the wind instruments were equal to the task, but the strings gave only a half audible hum. The piano passages were simply silence at such a distance, and with such a multitude between. When *"Hail Columbia"* closed the performance, all eyes waited for President *Grant* to appear, but it was about a quarter before eleven when he came upon the platform, apparently from the rear, for I did not discover him among the arriving guests.

Bishop *Simpson* began his prayer in a low voice, which grew clearer and stronger as he proceeded. It was an earnest and fervent utterance, and the vast crowd, very few of whom could hear anything of it, were respectfully silent, many who were far out of earshot uncovering their heads. But when the chorus rose, and the first word of *Whittier*'s hymn fell from a thousand lips, the pulse of the multitude began to beat. Strong, distinct and sweet, the lines floated far and wide on the soft air, not a word indistinguishable. Mr. *Paine*'s music seemed to me surprisingly fine. Mr. *Sidney Lanier,* who sat beside me, said, "It has the noble simplicity of an old Gregorian chant." Would that the poet could have been present! His earnest words never before entered so many souls, clad in such a glorious garb of sound. The impression was so deep and universal that the applause at its close became unwelcome to the ear.

Mr. *Welsh,* in making his presentation speech, was heard only in the immediate neighborhood of the platform. His tall, erect figure and dignified head, however, was well known to the people, and they gave him three cheers at the close.

I wish some of the critics who were made so unhappy by Mr. *Lanier*'s cantata could have heard it sung to Mr. *Dudley Buck*'s music. The words suffered a "sea-change" into another tongue; the stanzas relieved each other, and unexpected dramatic felicities were recognized by the mind through the ear. I never before heard a chorus sing with the pure and changeful expression of a single voice. The choruses in *Handel*'s oratorios, given at *Sydenham* twenty years ago, under *Da-Costa*'s direction, were surpassed by the performance of today. It was original in the perfection of the execution no less than in the conception of both poet and composer.

The effect upon the audience could not be mistaken. Mr. *Whitney* sang his bass solo,

> "Long as thine Art shall love true love,
> Long as thy Science truth shall know,
> Long as thine Eagle harms no Dove,
> Long as thy Law by law shall grow,

Long as thy God is God above,
Thy brother every man below,
So long, dear Land of all my love,
Thy name shall shine, thy fame shall glow!"

Every word, with its faintest modulation of expression, was distinctly heard by at least 15,000 persons. At the close, the applause was so great that the chorus, already underway, was suddenly stopped to allow an encore for the solo—a thing almost unprecedented on an occasion of the kind. At the end of the cantata, the thousand members of the chorus rose by one impulse, and gave three cheers—either for Mr. *Thomas,* Mr. *Buck* or Mr. *Whitney,* perhaps for all three. It was a thoroughly inspiring scene, and lent its fire to the remaining proceedings.

Gen. *Hawley* spoke in a chest-voice, so robust and well managed that I estimate he was heard by probably 8,000 of the audience. His address of presentation was received with tremendous cheering. Then President *Grant* arose and stepped to the front of the platform. He has grown quite stout of late, but looks well, and his face improved wonderfully when he smiled upon the crowd. There was a scattered, irregular fire of cheering until Gen. *Hawley* gave a signal with a wave of his arm, and the great multitude shouted together. The President read his reply from a printed copy, in an ordinary conversational tone. I was within twenty feet of him, and I could not catch a single word. When he pronounced the Exhibition opened, the signal was given. A flag ran up the staff on the *Main Building,* the chimes began, the cannon boomed from *George's Hill,* and the orchestra and chorus pealed forth the majestic *Hallelujah Chorus.* The strong harmonies of the last, however, drowned all other sounds— if, indeed, any one could think of listening for them. It was just noon; the sun was shining, the air was full of diffused light, and all nature, in breeze and foliage and play of colors, seemed to join in the jubilee.

THE PROCESSION

With the cessation of the chorus, Mr. *Dixey* took his stand, to arrange the order of the official procession through the buildings. Mr. *Goshorn* gave his arm to President *Grant,* who immediately gave his other arm to the Empress of Brazil. The Emperor followed with Mrs. *Grant.* There was, of course, no announcement of these chief personages; those that followed were summoned to their places. But the platform had become so crowded, and all the policemen so occupied in desperately holding back the struggling masses, that not even the diplomatic bodies could get into their proper places. The prescribed order of the procession was soon violated by eager American statesmen and their impatient ladies; presently members of the crowd which had besieged the Press, shutting out air and view, joined the current, and the line at last became so hopelessly mixed that I also trusted myself to it, much in advance of the proper place.

On entering the *Main Hall,* the distraction constantly increased. There were ropes drawn in some places; in others the exhibitors and their friends considerately kept their stand; but at every step there were accessions from somewhere, interruptions of the line of march, and finally a chaotic mixture, in which only the Presidential party was spared. The latter walked rapidly up the main aisle to the eastern end, then returned by the southern side aisle, taking a rapid glance at the American, Dutch, Brazilian and English departments. Externally, the American part was in tolerable order; but there is still a hideous waste of dirt, boards, packing paper and straw, extending the whole distance in its rear.

In the western half, France, Germany, Spain, Egypt, Switzerland, Norway and Japan were rapidly visited, and I believe all the Commissioners were duly greeted in passing. Before reaching the western entrance there was no longer a procession. Streams of impatient outsiders forced their way through the files of soldiers and poured into the Hall. The invited guests were separated, mixed, and tangled on every side, and only a stalwart guard of soldiers kept a little free space for the President, Emperor, and Centennial Commission.

I may say, generally, that the Exhibition is much further advanced than was that at Vienna on the opening day; that the show, while not quite so brilliant, is fully as varied and interesting, and that the spectacular effect is all that could be achieved in such a place.

The way across the open space to the *Machinery Hall* was kept clear by two files of soldiers, and when the party had entered the latter hall, the remainder of the task was accomplished without interruption. This was the closing, and, in many respects, the most interesting act of the opening ceremonies. In the center of the great hall Mr. *Corliss,* proud and satisfied, stood beside the colossal engine. After rapid inspection and the necessary instruction, President *Grant* and Emperor *Dom Pedro* took hold of the separate objects (I never could understand machinery, and don't know whether they were cranks, valves or wheels) and the force of 2000 horses was smoothly and silently exerted. North and South America started the machinery of the world.

THE FORMAL PROCEEDINGS

As the great orchestra, under the baton of *Theodore Thomas,* which was located over the north entrance to the main building, broke forth on the first mellow strains of *"The Washington March,"* the crowd settled in its demonstrations, and as the national airs followed good order prevailed, only broken occasionally with bursts of applause, as some patriotic or familiar tune was rendered. The following airs were rendered: *The Washington March;* Argentine Republic, (*Marche de la Republica*); Austria, *Gott erhalte Franz den Kaiser;* Belgium, *La Braban conne;* Brazil, *Hymno Brasilerira Nacional;* Denmark, *Volkslied—den tappre Landsoldat;* France, *La Marseillaise;* Germany, *Was ist des Deutschen Vaterland;* Great Britain, *God Save the Queen;* Italy, *Marcia del Re;* Netherlands, *Wic neerlandsch bloed;* Norway, *National hymn;* Russia, *National hymn;* Sweden, *Volksongen* (*Bevare Gud var Kung*); Switzerland, *Heil dir Helvetia;* Turkey, *March; Hail Columbia.*

At the conclusion of the orchestral selections, General *Hawley* came to the front of the platform and announced that the proceedings would be opened with prayer. He asked the people to remember the occasion and to exhibit to strangers the usual good nature and conduct of an American crowd. The Rev. Bishop *Simpson* then came forward and delivered a prayer, a large portion of the immense assemblage listening with bowed heads and respectful attention.

The chorus of a thousand voices then rendered Whittier's beautiful hymn, which we have heretofore published.

JOHN WELSH'S ADDRESS

John Welsh, President of the *Centennial Board* of *Finance,* presented the buildings to the *United States Centennial Commission* in the following words:

"Mr. President and Gentlemen of the United States Centennial Commission:

In the presence of the government of the United States, and of the several distinguished bodies by whom we are surrounded, and in behalf of the *Centennial Board* of *Finance,* I greet you.

"In readiness at the appointed time, I have the honor to announce to you that, under your supervision and in accordance with the plans fixed and established by you, we have erected the buildings belonging to us, and have made all the arrangements devolving on us necessary for the opening of the *"International Exhibition."* We hereby now formally appropriate them for their intended occupation; and we hold ourselves ready to make all further arrangements that may be needed for carrying into full and complete effect all the requirements of the acts of Congress relating to the Exhibition.

"For a like purpose, we also appropriate the buildings belonging to the *State* of *Pennsylvania* and the *City* of *Phildelphia,* erected by us at their bidding to wit: *Memorial Hall, Machinery Hall* and *Horticultural Hall.* These and other substantial cfferings stand as the evidence of their patriotic cooperation. To the *United States* of *America,* through Congress, we are indebted for the aid which crowned our success.

"In addition to those which I have just referred, there are other beautiful and convenient edifices, which have been erected by the representatives of foreign nations, by State authority, and by individuals, which are also devoted to the purposes of the Exhibition.

"Ladies and Gentlemen . . . If in the past we have met with disappointments, difficulties and trials, they have been overcome by a consciousness that no sacrifice can be too great which is made to honor the memories of those who brought our nation into being. This commemoration of the events of 1776 excites our present gratitude. The assemblage here today of so many foreign representatives uniting with us in this reverential tribute is our reward.

"The beauty and utility of the contributions will this day be submitted to your inspection by the managers of this Exhibition. We are glad to know that a view of specimens of the skill of all nations will afford to you unalloyed pleasure, as well as yield to you a valuable practical knowledge of so many of the remarkable results of the wonderful skill existing in enlightened communities.

Within the present limits of this great park were the homes of eminent patriots of that era, where *Washington* and his associates received generous hospitality and able counsel. You have observed the surpassing beauty of the situation placed at our disposal. In harmony with all this fitness is the liberal support given the enterprise by the State, the city and the people individually.

"In the name of the United States you extended a respectful and cordial invitation to the governments of other nations to be represented and to participate in this Exhibition. You know the very acceptable terms in which they reponded, from even the most distant regions. Their commissioners are here, and you will soon see with what energy and brilliancy they have entered upon this friendly competition in the arts of peace.

"It has been the fervent hope of the Commission that during this festival year the people from all states and sections, of all creeds and churches, all parties and classes, burying all resentments, would come up together to this birthplace of our liberties to study the evidence of our resources; to measure the progress of a hundred years, and to examine to our profit the wonderful products of other lands; but especially to join hands in perfect fraternity, and promise the God of our fathers that the new century shall surpass the old in the true glories of civilization. And furthermore, that from the association here of welcome visitors from all nations there may result not alone great benefits to invention, manufactures, argiculture, trade and commerce, but also stronger international friendships and more lasting peace.

"Thus reporting to you, Mr. President, under the laws of the government and the usage of similar occasions, in the name of the *United States Centennial Commission,* I present to your view the *International Exhibition* of 1876."

THE EXHIBITION DECLARED OPEN

Immediately following General *Hawley*'s speech President *Grant* discharged the last formal act of the simple yet dignified ceremonies by making proclamation of the eventful fact of the opening of the *International Exhibition.* The remarks of the President, like all of the other speeches of the day, were in writing, and at intervals were applauded with great spirit. The following is the address:

"MY COUNTRYMEN:—It has been thought appropriate upon this Centennial occasion to bring together in *Philadelphia,* for popular inspection, specimens of our attainments in the industrial and fine arts, and in literature, science and philosophy, as well as in the great business of agriculture and commerce.

"That we may the more thoroughly appreciate the excellencies and deficiencies of our achievements, and also give emphatic expression to our earnest desire to cultivate the friendship of our fellow members of this great family of nations, the enlightened agricultural, commercial and manufacturing people of the world have been invited to send hither corresponding specimens of their skill, to exhibit on equal terms, in friendly competition with our own. To this invitation they have generally responded. For so doing we render our hearty thanks.

"We congratulate you on the occurrence of this day. Many of the nations have gathered here in peaceful competition. Each may profit by the association. This Exhibition is but a school; the more thoroughly its lessons are learned the greater will be the gain, and when it shall have closed if by that study the nations engaged in it shall have learned respect for each other, then it may be hoped that veneration for Him who rules on high will become universal, and the angels' song once more be heard:

"Glory to God in the highest,
And on earth peace, good will towards men."

General *Hawley* said: "The Commission accepts the trust with grateful and fraternal acknowledgement of the great work performed by the *Board* of *Finance.*"

The cantata composed by *Sidney Lanier,* of Georgia—music by *Dudley Buck,* of *Connecticut*—was then given by the choir, the rendition of the piece including a basso solo by *Myron W. Whitney,* of *Boston,* who was much applauded.

THE PRESENTATION OF THE EXHIBITION

The formal presentation of the Exhibition to the President of the United States was made by Gen. *Joseph R. Hawley,* President of the *United States Centennial Commission.* The following is a literal report of his speech as delivered:

"Mr. President:—Five years ago the President of the United States declared it fitting that "the completion of the first century of our national existence should be commemorated by an exhibition of the natural resources of the country and their development, and of its progress in those arts which benefit mankind," and ordered that an exhibition of American and foreign arts, products and manufactures should be held, under the auspices of the Government of the United States, in the city of *Philadelphia,* in the year 1876. To put into effect the several laws relating to the Exhibition, the *United States Centennial Commission* was constituted, composed of two commissioners from each state and territory, nominated by their respective governors and appointed by the President. The Congress also created our auxiliary and associate corporation, the *Centennial Board* of *Finance,* whose unexpectedly heavy burdens have been nobly borne. A remarkable and prolonged disturbance of the finances and industries of the country has greatly magnified the task; but we hope for a favorable judgment of the degree of success attained.

"July 4, 1873, this ground was dedicated to its present uses. Twenty-one months ago this *Memorial Hall* was begun. All the other 180 buildings within the enclosure have been erected within twelve months. All the buildings embraced in the plans of the Commission itself are finished. The demands of applicants exceeded the space, and strenuous and continuous efforts have been made to get every exhibit ready in time.

"By general consent the Exhibition is appropriately held in the *City* of *Brotherly Love.* Yonder, almost within your view, stands the venerated edifice wherein occurred the event this work is designed to commemorate, and the hall in which the first Continental Congress assembled.

"One hundred years ago our country was new and but partially settled. Our necessities have compelled us to chiefly expend our means and time in felling forests, subduing prairies, building dwellings, factories, ships, docks, warehouses, roads, canals, machinery, etc., etc. Most of our schools, churches, libraries, and asylums have been established within a hundred years. Burdened by these great primal works of necessity, which could not be delayed, we yet have done what this Exhibition will show in the direction of rivalling older and more advanced nations in law, medicine and theology; in science, literature, philosophy and the fine arts. While proud of what we have done, we regret that we have not done more. Our achievements have been great enough, however, to make it easy for our people to acknowledge superior merit wherever found.

"And now, fellow citizens, I hope a careful examination of what is about to be exhibited to you will not only inspire you with a profound respect for the skill and taste of our friends from other nations, but also satisfy you with the attainments made by our own people during the past one hundred years. I invoke your generous cooperation with the worthy Commissioners to secure a brilliant success to this *International Exhibition,* and to make the stay of our foreign visitors—to whom we extend a hearty welcome—both profitable and pleasant to them.

"I declare the *International Exhibition* now open."

At the close of the President's remarks the signal was given, and flags were hoisted on all the buildings, the steam whistle sounded, guns boomed, and the grand inaugural of America's hundredth-year celebration was complete. The crowd then began to disperse, although those about the grandstand remained until the dignitaries took up their line of march for a general inspection of the buildings. The President and *Dom Pedro* headed the procession, the latter walking with Mrs. *Grant,* and the President with the Empress. Then followed the public men, Governors of *Massachuetts, New Jersey, Pennsylvania,* etc. Generals *Sherman* and *Sheridan,* with distinguished foreigners, ambassadors and officers of the army and navy. In a little while the outside platforms were deserted, and the various buildings filled with the late surging crowd, which might be estimated at over two hundred thousand people.

INCIDENTS OF THE OCCASION

The early sun scattered the clouds and rain, and the days' work began with an unfurling of the flags, which for weeks had been stored up for the opening day. A vivid imagination could not have pictured beforehand the display of bunting, which astonished even the citizens who had created the *Day* of *Flags* in *Philadelphia*—the first of January. Nearly every house showed its colors, and many bristled from roof to cellar with flags. There was hardly a residence which had not a pole on its roof or extending from its upper windows, to say nothing of the infinite number of little flags with which ingenious taste had adorned the fronts of the buildings. The principal business streets of the city vied with each other in their efforts to display the largest number of colors of each of the nations in the smallest possible space. *Chestnut Street* was conspicuous among its rivals in this respect. Standing almost head and shoulders above, the old *Independence Hall* showed $5,000 worth of bunting, and the *Public Ledger's* five stories of almost numberless windows must have had a thousand small flags as a fitting canopy for the statue of Franklin—its central and only piece of ornamentation.

He was a wise man who started for the Exposition grounds an hour sooner than had been his custom on other days, if his mode of conveyance was by street-car, or even by carriage. Although the gates for general visitors opened at 9 o'clock, the car terminal of the five lines of railway, which empty at the main entrances, were crowded as early as 6 o'clock. The exhibitors, who were let into the different buildings an hour or two before the general public or invited guests, of course made up this first throng; but by 7 o'clock people filled every car on every line, although the vehicles ran on one-minute and in some instances half-minute time. As the moment of opening the fair approached, the only way to get into any public conveyance at all was to catch it on the return trip and "ride around." Thus was presented the novel sight of full cars going down *Chestnut* and her parallel streets when the proper direction to the Centennial grounds was directly opposite.

In addition to the street cars and carriages gorging the streets leading to the goal of all the inhabitants of the great city, the military of the State and of the neighboring States seemed to have emptied themselves into the main thoroughfares, and *Broad Street* was dotted with regiments and companies and bedizened horsemen. These, with their accompanying crowds of lookers-on, made a sight the like of which one may never look upon again. As the visitor approached the grounds, either through the broad and beautiful roads in the Park, or by the gridironed streets of the city, the throng became denser and the gates more difficult of access. The *Pennsylvania Railroad* was bringing every hour 20,000 people, the *Reading Railroad* was running long trains from nearly the heart of the city every seven minutes, the street railways, the carry-alls, the carriages and the pedestrians, all contributed to fill the acres upon acres of space usually empty outside the 106 entrance gates with perfect "seas of humanity." The Centennial authorities had wisely placarded the enclosure with directions to the specially invited guests and press, so that their entrances were comparitively free from the long lines of people waiting for their turn to pass the turnstiles.

Although it had been heralded through the local press so often that the special instruction to the visitor to bring a fifty-cent note or piece for his admission had become a laughing matter, it was astonishing to see the crowd about the *Centennial Bank* windows, at which the dollar notes and two twenty-five-cent notes were changed into the admission fee of a fifty-cent note or piece. Even this embarrassment of riches with which those who had not heeded the injunction was taken advantage of by the speculators, and far above the other cries of guidebooks, official catalogues, "Gentlemen of the press this way," peanuts, etc., was the exremely original but in many cases gratifying announcement from a hundred throats within the very sound of the bank officers' voices, "Here you are, a fifty-cent note for seventy-five cents; save yourself the trouble of standing in line!" The police arrangements outside the gates were admirable, the Mayor's 1200 men having been supplemented by 500 specials. Many of these were strung all around the grand enclosure, and strong detachments placed at all the gates. So admirable indeed were these arrangements that the looker-on "on the outside" might have been there for an hour and he would not have seen a single disturbance, much less arrest, made. The gate keepers say their departments moved like clock-work, the people passed through without a single stoppage, the fifty-cent note provision requiring but a glance at the denomination and the motion of the hand to put the admission fee into a box.

By ten o'clock at least 200,000 men, women and children had crowded inside and dispersed themselves over the spacious grounds of 236 acres. The buildings proper did not open until noon, and the people, not of the 5000 invited guests or of the 1500 newspaper men, amused themselves by crowding up to the above-mentioned favored ones as they stood or sat on the grandstand between the *Main Building* and *Memorial Hall,* or else they scattered themselves everywhere over the broad well-paved walks along the lakes, or lined the main avenues to watch the soldiers and listen to the music of the many bands. Still others drew long sighs of relief at being fairly within the grounds after the long tedious ride, and sought out the seats in the shady places, or if not of frugal minds caught up the rolling chairmen, and were pushed around to see the sights until the booming of the great cannon, the ringing of the bells, and the simultaneous raising of the flags on all the flag staffs of the numerous buildings within the grounds told that the *Great International Exposition* of *America* had been formally opened.

THE MILITARY

One of the principal attractions in the city during the early part of the morning of course was the formation of the military, and as it had been previously announced that the division would escort President *Grant,* Governor *Rice* of

Massachusetts, Governor *Hartranft* and other distinguished visitors from their quarters, the crowd along the sidewalks resolved itself into a jam. The line began to form about 7:30 o'clock, on *Broad Street,* right resting on *Locust Street.*

The line moved off with creditable punctuality, all things considered, the muddy and slippery condition of the streets interfering materially with the marching. The parade moved out *Locust Street,* the troops being in the following order:

Troop Black Hussars, *Capt. I. Kleinz;* Washington Troop (of Chester county), *Capt. Matlack;* Keystone Battery, *Capt. Poulterer;* Second Brigade, United States Marines. *Brig. Gen. Thayer,* right resting on Spruce Street; Third Regiment N. G. of Pennsylvania, *Col. Maxwell;* State Fencibles, *Capt. Ryan;* Gray Invincibles, *Capt. Jones;* escorting the De Laney Guards of West Chester, *Capt. Hood;* First Brigade, *Col. R. Dale Benson* commanding, right resting on *South Street;* Second Regiment, N. G. of Pennsylvania, *Col. Peter Lyle;* First Regiment, N. G. Pennsylvania, *Lieut. Col. J. Ross Clark;* Eleventh Regiment, Tenth Division, N. G. of Pennyslvania, *Col. F. A. Tencate;* Company F, Fourth Regiment, N. G. of Penna., *Capt. Stetger;* Weccacoe Legion, *Capt. Denny;* Washington Grays, *Lieut. Lazarus;* Cadets of Pennsylvania Military Academy, Chester, *Lieut. Barnett,* Fifth U. S. Artillery, commanding.

At *Twenty-second* and *Walnut,* in front of Mr. *George W. Childs* house, the First brigade halted, admitting the City Troop escorting President *Grant* of the United States, Secretary *Fish, Governor Rice* of Massachusetts, and others, who were escorted by the Boston Cadets. The line then moved over the following route: *Twenty-second* to *Chestnut,* to *Thirty-second,* to *Market,* to *Lancaster Avenue,* to *Fortieth,* and entered the Exhibition grounds by the *Landsdowne* entrance.

THE THRONGS ABOUT THE BUILDINGS

After the President and the Emperor left the buildings and the official guests had dispersed, the multitude poured through all the departments in an unbroken stream for several hours. Although there were, according to the gate returns, considerably more than 200,000 people on the grounds, they spread themselves so rapidly through the various buildings that there was very little crowding except about the passage from the *Main Building* to *Machinery Hall;* and even there the pressure was soon relieved. Very few probably suspected that such a mighty multitude was moving about them, and it speaks volumes in praise of the police regulations that there was neither disorder nor even confusion. In fact, it was an eminently respectable and orderly multitude, largely composed of plain people from out of town, who highly appreciated some features of the show, but seemed to have an inadequate comprehension of the spectacle upon which it was their privilege to gaze. They blocked up the approaches to the Swedish Department, looking at the life-size figures in the national peasant costume, but they had no eyes for the exquisite silver filagree of

Norway close beside them. They gathered in amused groups around convex mirrors, laughing at the distortion of their faces, and whenever a person was found playing the piano, or music boxes were wound up, they settled down to have a good time. But the finest features of the fair seemed to be quite neglected. Those wonderfully beautiful ceramic courts in the English section were deserted. There were only two or three persons in front of the great show of Bohemian glass, and where Germany showed perhaps the most beautiful things in the whole Exhibition, the superb porcelain from the royal factory at Berlin, I found not a single spectator. To tell the truth, most of the many thousands who were in the hall between 5 and 6 o'clock seemed to be the class of people who make the fortunes of *Barnum*. They invaded the enclosed rooms and took possession of chairs and sofas, the exhibitors generally treating them with great courtesy; and they sat on Chinese porcelain as if it were only a lot of old blue beer kegs. After the first rush was over, indeed, one had a better chance to perceive the real elegance, brightness and variety of the Exhibition than had ever been afforded the most privileged visitor before. All packing cases were out of the way. There was no rubbish, except the guide books and soda water, in any of the principal passages or the courts opening off them. The showcases were at last uncovered, the flags and banners unfurled, the busy workmen at rest, and the exhibitors at leisure to answer questions. Beautiful as the scene had appeared to me in the morning during the last hour of preparation, it was tenfold more beautiful now, when the last touch had added a little color here and a ray of gold or silver there, and the blessing of repose had at last consecrated the work.

CLOSE OF THE DAY

No exact information could be obtained this evening at the *Department* of *Admissions* as to the number of people on the Exhibition grounds, but the officers in charge said that the estimate was that over 200,000 had paid at the gate, and that about 25,000 had come in on invitations, and on exhibitors, employers, and press passes. The attendance exceeded the most sanguine expectations. Fortunate were those who left the grounds early. Soon after 4 o'clock it began to rain, and the rush for the street cars was fearful. The three lines were totally inadequate to accomodate the crowd, and thousands of people were obliged to walk long distances through the muddy streets. The *Market Street Line* appeared to have broken down when most needed, for at five o'clock it had not a single car on its siding. In the morning the street cars failed almost as conspicuously to meet the demands upon them. Only passengers who lived near the town terminus could get even a chance to cling on to a strap. Before the cars had traversed one-third of the distance they ceased to stop for passengers. When people find out the conveniences offered at the *Reading* and *Pennsylvania Railroads*, the horse lines will not be so overtaxed.

There was much less of an illumination than was expected, especially along *Chestnut Street* and others in which the retail houses are located. The large wholesale places on *Market* and other streets seemed to have more enthusiastic owners, and the private residences made great displays of gaslight and bunting.

The feature of the evening in the social world is the reception which *George W. Childs* has given to the President and the Emperor and their suites. It was a most brilliant assemblage, consisting of all the greater dignitaries, foreign, national and local, who were at the grounds today. The Press of this and other states and countries, the Bar and Pulpit also being largely represented. It was probably the most distinguished party ever assembled in the parlors of any private gentleman in this country.

PANORAMIC VIEW OF CENTENNIAL EXHIBITION, FROM GEORGE'S HILL

The grounds were not quite ready on opening day; some debris was about and work on a few of the buildings was incomplete. Beyond the tent stood the large **California Building,** *where westerners liked to rendezvous; to the left and slightly back of the building stood the popular English house. "The* **English House** *is apparently of timber and mortar; but really this effect is secured by spiking strips of plank upon a uniform mortar surface...altogether, with its apparent solidity, its massive chimneys...it seems capable of giving shelter and all home comforts to two or three generations of tenants." The inside decoration of the house was described as "modest, but nevertheless rich...the dining-room, breakfast room, reception-room, office, parlor,--all have their open-mouthed fire-places... altogether it is a charming representative of a quiet, and sufficent old English country house..."*

Touring the Exhibits

Accommodation of Visitors

Main Exhibition Building

Memorial Hall

Machinery Hall

Agricultural Building

Midsummer Tour

Horticultural Hall

Annex Buildings

PLAN OF THE GROUNDS AND BUILDINGS OF THE CENTENNIAL EXHIBITION.
AT PHILADELPHIA, 1876

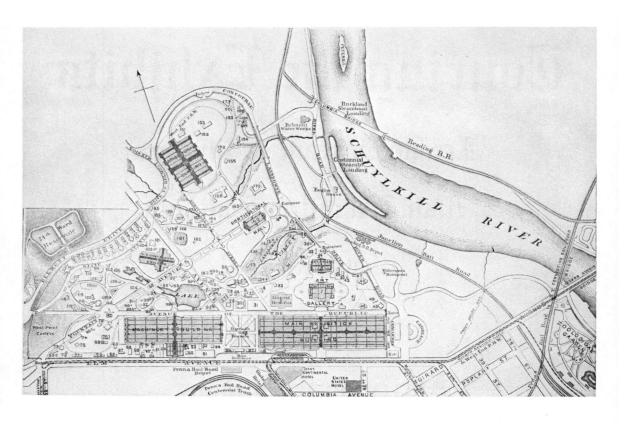

South-east Section.
1. Main Exhibition Building.
2. Memorial Hall (Art Gallery).
3. Annex to Art Gallery.
4. Photographic Gallery.
5. Carriage Building.
6. Centennial National Bank.
7. Public Comfort (clothes room).
8. Swedish School-house.
9. Penna. Educational Departm't.
10. Singer's Sewing Mach. Build'g.
11. Lafayette Restaurant.
12. Hunters' Camp.
13. Milk Dairy Association.
13A. Extension to Milk Dairy.
14. Bible Society.
15. Public Comfort.
16. Phila. Municipal Headquarters.
17. Soda Water.
18. Moorish Villa.
19. German Government Building.
20. Brazilian Government Build'g.
21. Kittredge & Co.
22. Soda Water.
23. Philadelphia "Times" Build'g.
24. Glass Factory.
25. Cigar Stand.
26. American Fusee Company.
27. Centennial Photographic Association.
28. Penna. R. R. Ticket Office.
29. Centennial Medical Departm't.
30. Judges' Hall.
31. Department of Public Comfort.
32. Japanese Government.
33. Kindergarten.
34. Soda Water.
35. Public Comfort Station.

36. Cigar Stand.
37. Stand Pipe.
38. French Government Building.
39. Stained Glass.
40. Vienna Bakery.
41. Bankers' Exhibit.
42. Empire Transportation Co.
43. Centennial Fire Patrol No. 2.
44. Portuguese Governm't Build'g.
45. Pavilion of French Art.
46. Burial Casket Building.
47. Public Comfort (clothes room).
48. Police Station.
49. Police Station.
49A. Music Stand.
49B. French Ceramic Pavilion.

South-west Section.
50. Machinery Hall.
51. Shoe and Leather Building.
52. British Boiler House.
53. Boiler House.
54. Corliss Boiler House.
55. Weimer's Furnace.
56. Boiler House.
57. Stokes & Parrish Machine Shop.
58. Boiler House.
59. Nevada Quartz Mill.
60. Gas Machine.
61. Yale Lock Company.
62. Brick Working Machine.
63. Storehouse.
64. Artesian Well.
65. Rock Drilling Machinery.
66. Jesse Starr & Son.
67. Gunpowder Pile Driver.
68. Automatic Railway.
69. Tiffany's Gas Machine.

70. Pennsylvania Railroad.
71. Engine House.
72. Emil Ross Saw Mill.
73. Gillinder & Son Glass Factory.
74. Annex (Saw Mill).
75. Saw Mill Boiler House.
76. Campbell Printing House.
77. Fuller, Warren & Co.
78. Liberty Stove Works.
79. Boston "Herald" and "Advertiser."
80. Catholic Total Abstinence Fountain.
81. Kiosque.
82. Turkish Cafe.
83. Pennsylvania State Building.
84. Pop Corn.
85. Rowell's Newspaper Build'g.
86. Lienard's Relief Plans.
87. Public Comfort Station.
88. Soda Water.
89. New York "Tribune."
90. French Restaurant.
91. Sons of Temperance Fount'n.
92. Colossal Arm of Liberty.
93. World's Ticket Office.
94. Catalogue Office.
95. Loiseau's Prepared Fuel Co.
96. Office Board of Finance.
97. Office U. S. Centennial Com.
98. Bartholdi's Fountain.
99. Jerusalem Bazaar.
99A. Vermont State Building.
99B. Chilian Machine Building.
99C. Police Station.
99D. Statue of Elias Howe.
99E. Columbus Monument.
99F. Averill Paint Company.

North-west Section.
100. U. S. Government Building.
101. United States Hospital.
102. United States Laboratory.
103. Cigar Stand.
104. Tent.
105. U. S. Signal Service.
106. Bishop Allen's Monument.
107. Soda Water.
108. Cigar Stand.
109. Canada Log House.
110. Arkansas State Building.
111. Spanish Building.
112. West Virginia State Building.
113. Spanish Government Build'g.
114. Spanish Government Build'g.
115. Japanese Building.
116. Mississippi State Building.
117. George's Hill Restaurant.
118. California State Building.
119. New York State Building.
120.
121. } British Government Build'gs.
122.
123. Public Comfort Station.
124. Tunisian Camp.
125. Centennial Fire Patrol No. 1.
126. Ohio State Building.
127. Indiana State Building.
128. Illinois State Building.
129. Wisconsin State Building.
130. Michigan State Building.
131. New Hampshire State Build'g.
132. Connecticut State Building.
133. Massachusetts State Building.
134. Delaware State Building.
135. Maryland State Building.
136. Tennessee State Building.

137. Iowa State Building.
138. Missouri State Building.
139. Block House.
140. Fire Patrol.
141. Rhode Island

North-east Section.
150. Agricultural Building.
151. Agricul'al Annex (Wagons).
152. "   "   (Pomology).
153. Brewers' Building.
154. Butter and Cheese Factory.
155. Tea and Coffee Press Build'g.
156. American Restaurant.
157. Kansas State Building.
158. Southern Restaurant.
159. New Jersey State Building.
160. Horticultural Hall.
161. Women's Pavilion.
162. Gliddon Guano Building.
163. New England Log House.
164. Pop-Corn.
165. Cigar Stand.
166. Cigar Stand.
167. Soda Water.
168. Bee Hives.
169. School House.
170. German Restaurant.
171. Virginia Building.
172. Boiler House.
173 to 183. Wind Mills.
184. Police Station.
185. Hay Packing.
186. Practical Farmers' Office.
187. Public Comfort Station.
188. Centennial Guards.
189. Public Comfort (cl. room).

KEY TO   GROUND PLAN.

THE EXHIBITION GROUNDS

———

ACCOMMODATION OF VISITORS

There are 17 Entrances to the Grounds.

The Gates are opened from 9 a.m. to 6 p.m. daily. Closed on Sunday.

Admission price—50 cents, payable in one note at the entrance gate. Includes everything seen in the Exhibition. Transfer tickets will be issued on request for cattle exhibits held outside the enclosure.

The *Centennial National Bank* located at convenient locations on the grounds, will afford the visitor every banking facility, and will deal in coin and exchange and cash letters of credit.

A narrow-gauge double-track steam railway is in operation for a tour of the grounds. A fixed fee of 5 cents per passenger will be charged.

Rolling chairs are for hire at designated stations within the grounds at 60 cents per hour or $4.50 per day (nine hours).

Chairs and benches within the principal Exhibition Buildings can be used at no charge to the visitor.

Soda-water fountains are conveniently located in the principal buildings, and at stands along the walks. Charge, per glass, 10 cents. The consumption of alcoholic beverages is prohibited on the grounds.

The *House* of *Public Comfort* includes separate parlors for the ladies and gentlemen; restrooms, barbershops, and coat and baggage rooms. Restrooms are also located at the entrance to all principal buildings.

OUTSIDE THE GROUNDS

Like fairs and exhibitions the world over, hawkers of snacks, cold drinks, and shoeshines were busy drumming up business.

RESTAURANTS

The *Great American Restaurant*—an ornamental two-story building with pavilions, verandas and beer garden. Decorated with fountains, statues, shrubbery, etc. Banqueting hall, private parlors, smokingrooms, bathrooms, barber shop. Bill of Fare or general table. German and French waiters.

Trois Frères Provençaux—two-story building overlooking lake. Hall, eight private saloons, and pavilions. French cusine.

Restaurant of the *South*—Smoking and readingrooms. Southern food. "Old Plantation Darkey Band" will furnish music and illustrate southern plantation scenes.

German Restaurant—three-acre beautiful garden. Musical entertainment. Seating capacity, 1500 guests. Bill of Fare or general table.

French Restaurant—"*La Fayette*." Two dining halls, seventeen private saloons. Parisian service. Bill of Fare (a la carte) only. Fine view of ground from upper balcony.

George's Hill Restaurant—Oriental style. Dining hall, smokingroom, ladies' dressingroom. Bill of Fare or general table. Dietary law of Israelites observed. Fine view of grounds from upper veranda.

The Dairy—Rustic building. Garden, shadetrees, shrubbery, with chairs and tables. Milk, cream, cheese, ice cream, pastries, fruit and berries for sale. Girls dressed as Swiss peasants in attendance.

Vienna Bakery and *Coffee House*—New York and Cincinnati. Specialties, "Chocolat à la Crême" and fresh Vienna bread. Sales Room.

THE GRAND ENTRANCE

The visitor who saw the **Centennial Exhibition** *for the first time would add to his treasure of lifetime memories. The sight of the third-of-a-mile buff and gold* **Main Building,** *standing in the bright sunshine, was majestic and unforgettable. Inside were the sights, smells, and wonders of the world.*

PROGRAMME OF EVENTS

SOCIETY MEETINGS, PARADES, REGATTAS, ETC.

American Master Mechanics Association, May 16.
Butchers' Parade, May 18.
Knights Templar (Masons), Annual Conclave, May 30.
Medical Society of Pennsylvania, May 31.
Knights Templar (Masons), Grand Parade, June 1.
American Medical Association, June 6.
Order of Good-Templars, Special Gathering, June 13.
American Society of Civil Engineers, June 13.
Sons of Temperance, Meeting of National Division, June 14.
American Institute of Mining Engineers, June.
International Yacht Race (New York Harbor), June 22,23, 26.
American Kennel Club, June.
International Series of Cricket Matches, June and September.
American Protestant Association, Parade, June 29.
Grand Army of the Republic, National Encampment, June 30.
Grand Army of the Republic, Parade, July 1.
Congress of Authors in Independence Hall, July 2.
Parade of Military Organizations, and Special Ceremonies, July 4.
Parade of Catholic Total Abstinence Societies and Dedication of Fountain, July 4.
United American Mechanics, Parade, July 8.
International Scottish Games, August 14 and 15.
Convention of North American Caledonian Association, August 16.
Knights of Pythias, Parade, August 22.
International Rowing Regatta, August 20 to September 15.
International Rifle Matches, September 12.
International Medical Congress, September 4.
Independent Order of Odd-Fellows, Parade, September 20.
National Pomological Society, September 11.
Firemen's Parade, September.
American Arboricultural Society.
Sons of Temperance, Grand Division of Pennsylvania, October 25.

GRAND CEREMONIES ON EXHIBITION GROUNDS, JULY 4

On July 4, 1876, there will be, under the auspices of the *United States Centennial Commission*, an old-fashioned celebration of the day. The President of the United States will preside. *Bishop Stevens*, the ecclesiastical successor of the first chaplain of the Continental Congress, will invoke the Divine blessing. *Richard Henry Lee*, of Virginia, grandson of the *Richard Henry Lee* who moved the Declaration, will read the *Declaration of Independence. Bayard Taylor* will read a poem. Hon. *William M. Evarts*, of *New York*, will deliver the address. In the evening there will be a magnificent display of fireworks. The entire week will be given up to military and other displays.

THE AMERICAN RESTAURANT AND AGRICULTURAL HALL, FROM THE HORTICULTURAL BUILDING

The **American Restaurant** *was run by two enterprising and experienced Philadelphia restauranteurs. Everything was American--silverware, tables, cooking utensils, etc., all of native manufacture. The food was the usual American cuisine - boarding-house style or bill of fare. The large garden area around the restaurant consisted of fountains, shrubbery, statues, and the concert music was American. But the shrewd proprietors made one exception--thewaiters were German and French.*

MEMORIAL HALL DEPOT, TERMINAL POINT ON THE RAIL TOUR

The three mile double track miniature railroad was a delight to the fair-goer, if for no other reason than to give tired feet a rest. One visitor wrote: "W took our first ride on the narrow-gauge railroad, of which the locomotive with its train of gay open cars coughs and writhes about the grounds in every direction, with a station at each of the great buildings. I believe the railroad has awakened loathing in some breasts, and that there has been talk of trying to have it abolished. But I venture to say this will never be done, and in fact I do not see how the public could get on without it. The fare is five cents for the whole tour or from any one point to another; the ride luxuriously refreshing, and commands a hundred charming prospects. To be sure the cars go too fast, but that saves time; and I am not certain that the flagmen at the crossings are sufficiently vigilant to avert accidents."

The

Main Exhibition

Building

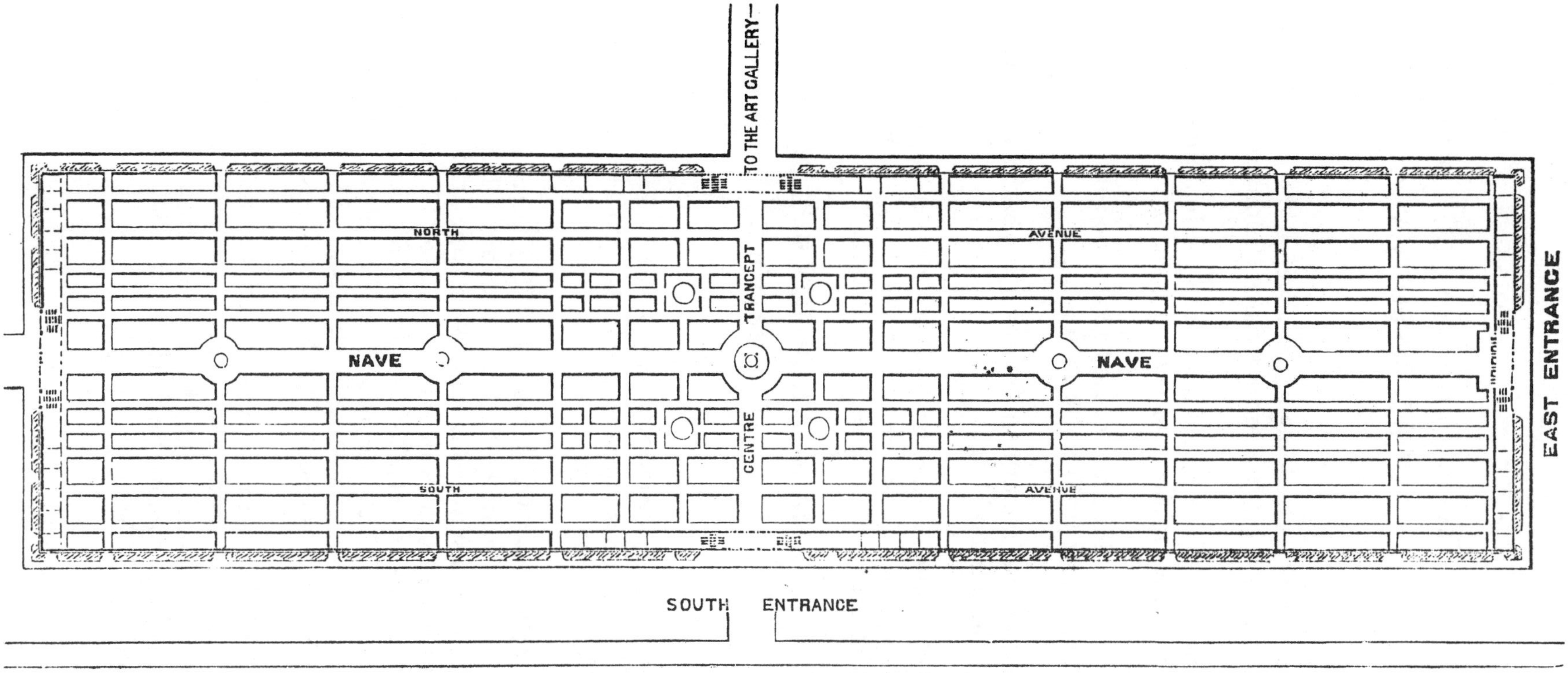

EAST ENTRANCE

NAVE

AVENUE

AVENUE

TO THE ART GALLERY—

CENTRE TRANSEPT

NORTH

SOUTH

NAVE

SOUTH ENTRANCE

ELM AVENUE

GROUND PLAN, MAIN EXHIBITION BUILDING,

MAIN EXHIBITION BUILDING
TOURIST INFORMATION

Visitors can enter this building under cover at the east Main Entrance (from carriages) or at the south Main Entrance (from street cars).

An excellent view of the whole interior of the building can be obtained from the small balconies in the four central towers.

The countries exhibiting are located geographically in sections running crosswise of the building from north to south.

A visitor must travel about 11 miles traversing both sides of each avenue to see the exhibits in this building.

The *Foreign Commissioners* have offices adjacent to the exhibits of their respective countries. The *Centennial Executive Offices* will be found on the second floors at the north side of this building.

MAIN EXHIBITION BUILDING
EXHIBITIONS

DEPARTMENT 1.—MINING AND METALLURGY. Classes 100-109. Minerals, ores, stones, mining products. 110-119. Metallurgical Products. 130-129. Mining Engineering.

DEPARTMENT II.—MANUFACTURES. Classes 200-205. Chemical Manufactures. 206-216. Ceramics, Pottery, Porcelain, Glass. 217-227. Furniture, etc. 228-234. Yarns and Woven Goods of Vegetable or Mineral Materials. 235-241. Woven and Felted Goods of Wool, etc. 242-249. Silk and Silk Fabrics. 250-257. Clothing, Jewelry, etc. 258-264. Paper, Blank Books, Stationery. 265-271. Weapons, etc. 272-279. Medicine, Surgery, Prothesis. 280-284. Hardware, Edge-Tools, Cutlery, and Metallic Products. 285-291. Fabrics of Vegetable, Animal, or Mineral Materials. 292-296. Carriages, Vehicles, and Accessories.

DEPARTMENT III.—EDUCATION AND SCIENCE. Classes 300-309. Educational Systems, Methods, and Libraries. 310-319. Institutions and Organizations. 320-329. Scientific and Philosophical Instruments and Methods. 330-339. Engineering, Architecture, Maps, etc. 340-349. Physical, Social, and Moral Condition of Man.

**MAIN BUILDING FROM SOUTHEAST TOWER,
LOOKING NORTHWEST**

The interior woodwork of the roof was washed with two coats of light pearl gray and decorated with stenciling; the ironwork was painted in buff and picked out with crimson; the pendants were crimson, blue, and gold. The interior side work in the building was also painted in colors--several shades of olive green decorated with crimson, blue, and gold. All clear glass, exposed to the sun, was tinted with an opaque wash to give the effect of stained glass. To the left an exhibit from **Germany,** *to the center and right* **India** *and* **Canada.**

MAIN BUILDING FROM EAST END

"Hardware forms a most prominent display, and the exhibits for building and household use from the United States are remarkable for variety, beauty of design and artistic finish, surpassing all those from foreign countries in these points." Locks had been an American specialty since the London Exhibit of 1851. In edge-tools the United States remained superior, and the American axe had a worldwide reputation. The hand tools for carpenters showed the inventive genius of the yankee. "In jewelry, watches and silverware the United States makes a most excellent exhibit, and in reference to watches, has caused great consternation among the Swiss manufacturers..." "In glass, however, after the rich colors and manifold lovely forms of the foreign exhibits, we were cold and gray...I heard that the show of book-making did us great honor. The exhibit of minerals was very large giving evidence of United States possessing great mineral wealth."

MAIN BUILDING FROM EAST GALLERY

The United States exhibit of silk and wool fabrics outrivaled that of the cotton manufacturers. Also included in the silk exhibit were elegant laces, ribbons, military trimmings, and threads.

EGYPTIAN FURNITURE AND VASES, MAIN BUILDING

"We move on, passing the Egyptian Department with its enclosure modeled after an old temple of the Nile. Peeping in, we ask after the Sphinx and mummies, to the evident disfavor of the gentleman in fez whom we address..." At the rear of the section three large bookcases in black and gold, peculiarly decorated, contained many books printed in Arabic. Also interesting were ancient manuscripts.

CRYSTAL WARE, MAIN BUILDING, CENTER AISLE, EAST END

The James Green *and* **Nephew, Thames Cut Glass Works, England,** *had a very large and beautiful display of cut-glassware. "One grand crystal chandelier, 7 by 15 feet, valued at $5,000. A pair of beautiful candelabras, $1,200. A set of wall lights, $800. One glass goblet, very delicately cut, $1,000; and another, still more elaborate in design, $150. Decanters per pair, $250. The entire exhibit worth $50,000.*

FARINA ARTISTIC CERAMICS CO. EXHIBIT, MAIN BUILDING

"The **Italian Department,** *to any one who knows what Italy's wealth in objects of art is, seems--with some single exceptions--a rather poverty-stricken effort of bric-a-brackishness. It presents a huddled, confused appearance; it is a shop where the prices asked are worthy of the "Trois Freres" themselves. The exhibit contained Roman and Florentine mosaics, cabinets, bronze, statuary, and furniture. At the northern end was a considerable display of book publications. There are some few samples of exquisite Italian printing, but the most is ordinary work...A Messina manufacturer, Welbatus sends one of the finest sets of heavy blank-book bindings in the Exhibition, huge journals in full calf, with solid metal mountings and clasps."*

103

MAIN BUILDING, CENTER AISLE, LOOKING NORTHEAST

To the left of the aisle, the **British Empire** *exhibits featured a wide variety of articles. Among the* **Australian** *exhibits were kangaroo leathers, strong and soft, saddles of Sydney leather, wools, and many minerals. Also shown were exhibits of sugars, tobacco, wheat, wines, and many canned fruits and vegetables. The* **Victoria** *exhibit included cases of cocoons and silks, threads, a case of butterflies and bugs [the latter proved unfavorable]. Also shown were "beautiful birds," black swans, etc. Fur and feather garments, wool rugs and mats, were especially fine. Patrons of the fair were attracted to two cases of gold nuggets which had a total value of $146,180. In the foreground, left, the* **Argentine Republic,** *near the west entrance, exhibited native ores, ingots and specimens of silver filigree, other ores and minerals, and petroleum from native springs.*

BELGIUM FURNITURE, MAIN BUILDING, NORTHEAST CORNER

The exhibit featured carved work. "Some fine specimens. Goyers Bros., of Louvain, furnish an old-fashioned pulpit with sounding board, and large panels on which were carved, very elegantly, Scriptural scenes. Price $4,000. Other wooden mantles, sideboards, cabinets. On closest examination, delicately carved."

MAIN BUILDING, TRANSEPT FROM SOUTHWEST TOWER

For those who passed through the Main Building in the pleasant days of May and June, it was delightful to hear the strains from Gilmore's Band [music platform, foregroung] or to hear the music from "the grand organ swelling up and dying away in the distance."

FROM THE GRANDSTAND LOOKING NORTHWEST, CENTER OF BUILDING

Elkington & Co., Manufacturing Silversmiths, London, Liverpoor, and Manchester. *"The exhibit displays a very rich assortment of various designs in repousse, cloisonne, and champ-leve enamels. The Helicon Vase is a masterpiece of art in repousse silver and steel, damascened in gold; valued at $30,000 gold. It is devoted to the apotheosis of Music and Poetry. The subjects of the Milton shield are taken from Paradise Lost, and strikingly and faithfully delineated. Value $15,000. The exhibit in Main Building is valued at $750,000."*

MAIN BUILDING, CENTER AISLE, LOOKING EAST

To the right, upper middle, exhibits from China featured curious carvings and huge porcelain vases. In the adjoining Japanese exhibit were many interesting books--odd and beautiful. The Peruvian exhibit, lower right, had a neat bookcase which contained both books and cigars.

PORCELAIN WARE, JAPANESE COURT

"Adjoining the bronze vases, on the main aisle, are the ceramics. Upon each side of the entrance to this department are massive vases; two of figured blue ware, and two of wares highly decorated in gold. There are several vases shown, which are remarkable for their size...Also, large bowls and tea-services, painted in designs peculiar to the country...In an adjoining case we find fan-shaped trays, and beautiful vases of a deep blue color. Facing upon the side aisle, are two large exhibits...elaborately ornamented in gold. In one, the background is mostly of a fine red...Adjoining there, is a large assortment of stoneware, of two shades of blue, in attractive designs..."

ITALIAN SECTION, MAIN BUILDING

"Venice sent a number of exquisite specimens of her glassware, and also some beautiful mosaics and corals. A prominent feature of this collection consisted of handsome mirrors of all sizes, which were in the best style of Venetian workmanship. There is also a pretty exhibit of pottery and majolica ware. It is not very large, but very attractive. Alongside of it were a number of statues, statuettes and busts in terra-cotta and baked clay."

ITALIAN DEPARTMENT

A young sculptor of Milan, Donato Barcaglia, sent to the Exposition a number of groups. Amount them was one entitled Fleeting Time, which consisted of two life-size figures in marble, it contradicts all our old ideas of the decorum of sculpture. It seems like fan painting petrified unkindly into stone. But the new school is determined to show it can indicate all the effects of painting."

Memorial Hall

and

Art Gallery Annex

MEMORIAL HALL AND ART GALLERY ANNEX
TOURIST INFORMATION

Each exhibit is numbered and information can be obtained by referring to similar numbers in the official catalogue of Exhibition.

When works of art are for sale, purchasers should bear in mind that no article can be removed until after the close of the Exhibition, November 10, 1876.

The visitor will find on exhibition the works of all the leading artists of the world. The committees of selection of the different nations have selected from the numerous works of art submitted to them, those they considered as best representing the art culture of their country. The best works of each country of the Old World have been taken, and placed in the main gallery of *Memorial Hall* and will be opposite, for close comparison, with the works of the most eminent artists of the United States, thus forming a most interesting exhibition.

MEMORIAL HALL AND ART GALLERY ANNEX
EXHIBITIONS

DEPARTMENT IV—ART. Classes 400-409. Sculpture. (In stone, metal, wood, iron, etc.) 410-419. Painting. (In oil and water colors on canvas, porcelain, enamel, metals, etc.) 420-429. Engraving and Lithography. 430-439. Photography (including photolithographs). 440-449. Industrial and Architectural Designs, Models and Decorations. 450-459. Decorations with Ceramic and Vitreous Materials; Mosaic and Inlaid Work.

MEMORIAL HALL

Memorial Hall *was erected as a permanent building on the most commanding portion of the great* **Lansdowne Plateau,** *standing 116 feet above the river. The Renaissance style of architecture was represented, but* **Wilson,** *the engineer, felt that there was a lack of harmony in the proportions and that the dome should have been larger and higher.* **William Dean Howells** *wrote: "The Art Hall, which is otherwise conventionally well enough, is disfigured by the colossal bronzes at the entrance." The bronzes referred to had been rejected by the* **Grand Opera House, Vienna,** *several years before. Near the building, on either side, stood two bronzes--to the right,* **Wolf's Dead Lioness,** *and on the left,* **Mead's** *group of* **The Navy** *[for the* **Lincoln Monument** *at* **Springfield, Illinois).** *The three huge arched main-entrance doorways were connected on each side by groined arch arcades with corner pavilions. In the rear of these arcades were open coutrs, paved and ornamented with fountains and plants intended for statuary. Under the dome of the building was the grand central hall, and east and west of this were the two main picture galleries. The central hall lighting was from the dome, the main picture galleries, the roof, and the smaller rooms by side windows. The Art Annex Building--a plain brick building, north of* **Memorial Hall,** *was built at the last moment to provide more space for the vast collections sent from many countries to the Exhibition.*

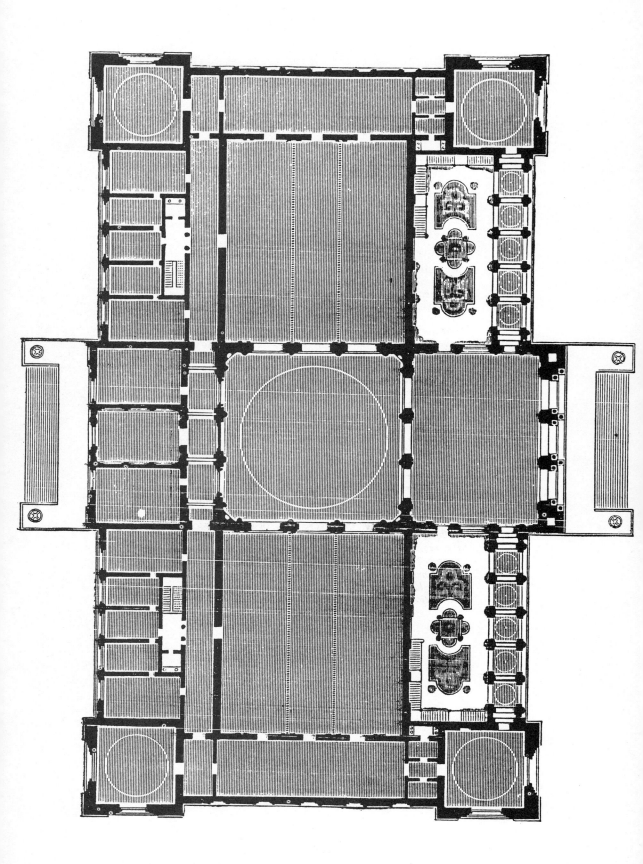

ITALIAN DEPARTMENT

"The show of sculpture within seems to have been almost entirely left to the country men of Michelangelo, who are here reposing, for the most part, upon his laurels." Although Americans were somewhat disappointed in the art Italy had sent to the Exhibition, that Feeling disappeared when the great collection of Signor Alessandro Castellani was viewed. The extremely valuable collection of 2,000 objects dated back to the pre-historic ages.

AMERICAN DEPARTMENT

In touring the Art Hall, William Dean Howells observed: "We had certainly no cause, considering all things, to be ashamed of the show of American paintings in comparison even with many of the English, and still less with those of other nations. There were not many positively poor, and there were many strikingly good, especially landscapes painted with sympathy, and portraits painted with character...You felf that American art had made vast advances on the technical side, but that it lacked what English art has got from its intimate association with literature..." The art exhibit by the United States was very large, about one-third of the entire collection. Of the 688 American oil paintings represented, 220 were imaginative and composition; 150 portraits; 187 landscapes; 15 animals; 15 interior views; 3 fish; 39 marine; 21 flower; 20 city views; 7 still life; 1 fruit; 3 miniature; 1 poultry; 15 historical; 2 birds; 1 vegetable. In addition to water colors were engravings and etchings on steel and copper, architectural designs and sculpture.

Machinery Hall

MACHINERY HALL
TOURIST INFORMATION

The east entrance on *Belmont Avenue* is the principal approach from the *Steam Railroad Depot* and from the street cars.

The west entrance is adjacent to *George's Hill* where a fine view can be had of the entire exhibition.

The 1400 horsepower *Corliss* engine is in the center of the building and is capable of driving the entire shafting necessary to run all of the machinery exhibits. The main lines of the shafting extend almost the entire length of the building; counter-shafts extend from the aisles into the avenues at necessary points.

The visitor can see the machinery of all nations in actual operation. Sample products can be purchased and removed if desired.

The annex for hydraulic machines has a tank 144 feet long, 60 feet wide, and a depth of 8 feet where hydraulic machinery will be exhibited in full operation. At the south end of the tank there is a spectacular waterfall 35 feet high and 40 feet long. The water comes from the tank and is supplied by the pumps on exhibition.

MACHINERY HALL
EXHIBITIONS

DEPARTMENT V—MACHINERY. Classes 500-509. Machines, Tools, etc., of Mining, Chemistry, etc. 510-519. Machines and Tools for working Metal, Wood, and Stone. 520-529. Machines and Implements of Spinning, Weaving, etc. 530-539. Machines, etc. used in Sewing, Making Clothing, etc. 540-549. Machines for Printing, Making Books, Paper Working, etc. 550-559. Motors, Power Generators, etc. 560-569. Hydraulic and Pneumatic Apparatus. 570-579. Railway Plant, Rolling Stock, etc. 580-589. Machinery used in Preparing Agricultural Products. 590-599. Aerial, Pneumatic, adapted to the requirements of the Exhibition.

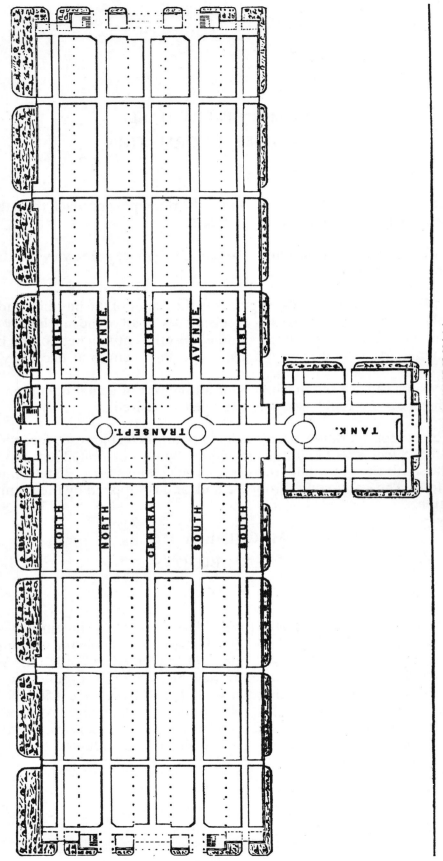

GROUND PLAN—MACHINERY HALL.

THE SCALE EXHIBIT

"The exhibit presents goods finely finished in every detail, though not so elaborately decorated as many shown elsewhere." The **Improved Howe Scales (Brandon Manufacturing Co.)** *displayed was valued at $20,000. One scale featured a platform covered with plate glass, so the fair-goer could see the working parts in operation.* **Fairbanks,** *probably the largest scale maker in the world, displayed an interesting variety of models ranging from the small laboratory type to the very heavy railroad scale. Among the many specialty scale makers* **John Chatillon and Sons** *exhibited neatly made fish and grocers' scales.* **Charles Reinhardt** *displayed a neat glass case of fascinating gold and diamond weighing devices.*

MACHINERY HALL, FROM MAIN BUILDING, EAST ENTRANCE

A broad asphalt avenue united the terminal facades of the **Main Building** *and* **Machinery Hall.** *The triangular spaces at the intersecting avenues were turfed and dressed with shrubbery. The central fountain, where all the avenues met, was made of bronze--the work of the French sculptor,* **Auguste Bartholdi.** *"Three colossal nymphs of exquisite form upbear a wide circular shield, into which the water falls from other figures, while ten lamps held up by as many beautiful arms shed light at night from their gas globes. The fountain is twenty feet in diameter, and about forty feet high." In the distance the tall skeleton observation tower could be seen on* **George's Hill** *[center]--one of the many private enterprises brought to the centennial and one of the most costly.* **"Sawyer's Improved Observatory,"** *built of expensive boiler iron, had a main shaft 200 feet high with an 8 feet diameter at the bottom, tapering to 3 feet at the top. At the top of the shaft was a platform about 20 feet in diameter, surrounded by a strong iron rail and covered with a wire netting to prevent accidents. The cable car carried 40 passengers comfortably. Fares were 25 cents for adults and 10 cents for children. At the bottom of the tower was an ornamental cottage used for a waiting room. Here picnicing parties could sit at benches and tables.*

LOOKING SOUTH FROM EAST END

"The display of machinery is greatly in excess of anything at previous exhibitions, and the United States is far ahead of any other country." Still, no American could view the **Cannon King's** *exhibit as the* **Alfred Krupp** *of the* **Krupp Works** *of Germany was called, without a feeling of awe. The monstrous 26¼ foot gun weighed 57¼ tons and could hurl a shot of more than a half a ton. The heavy cannon had not been in place on opening day due to the difficulties encountered in bringing it from the wharf to the exhibition grounds.*

TRANSEPT LOCOMOTIVES, PRINTING PRESSES, ETC., CENTER OF BUILDING WHERE STOOD THE GIANT CORLISS STEAM ENGINE

Nowhere on the Exhibition grounds could Americans thrill to patriotic pride as when they saw the railroad locomotive section in the center of **Machinery Hall.** *America led the world in railroading; their engines were the best and were in great demand for export. Air brakes and automatic couplers were standard equipment. The big names and shapes of locomotive manufacturing were on exhibit: the* **Baldwin** *works had five first-class engines and a mining locomotive. The celebrated high-wheel, fast* **Rodgers** *locomotive of* **Danforth, Dickson, Porter** *and* **Bell,** *and others.* **Brooks Locomotive Works** *had furnished the narrow gauge engine for the circular railroad on the Centennial grounds.*

SOUTH AISLE. PUMPS, KNITTING MACHINERY, BELTS AND SHAFTING, HYDRAULICS, ETC., SECTION

"Woman's skill was better represented in the **Machinery Hall** *than in her own Pavilion; there she was everywhere seen in operation and superintendence of the most complicated mechanisms, and showed herself in the character of a worker of unsurpassed intelligence,"* *wrote* **William Dean Howells** *on a visit to the exhibition. Amid the noisy bustle of large machinery, on the south aisle, stood the* **Brickford Knitting Machine** *booth where the visitor could tarry a minute or two to watch a young lady, who was entirely blind, do "the most perfect work on one of these little machines." Elsewhere in the Hall, a young lady operated the* **Radiant Flat Iron,** *an implement in whose hollow frame burnt a gas-flame blown hotter by a draft of air.*

The Agriculture

Bulding

THE AGRICULTURE BUILDING
TOURIST INFORMATION

The articles on exhibition are arranged by countries. A very interesting comparison of the different styles of agricultural implements can be made, as twenty foreign countries, and all of the States are exhibited.

There are extensive and interesting exhibits of agricultural machines in active operation, comprising everything used on farm or plantation, in tillage, harvesting, or in preparation for the market; manufactured foods of all kinds, and all varities of fish with improved appliances for fish culture.

The provisions made in the Department are the most complete ever attempted.

THE AGRICULTURAL BUILDING
EXHIBITIONS

DEPARTMENT VI—AGRICULTURE. Classes 600-609. Agriculture and Forest Products. 610-619. Pomology—Fruits from all parts of the world. 620-629. Agricultural Products. 630-639. Land Animals. 640-649. Marine Animals, Fish-culture and Apparatus. 650-664. Animal and Vegetable Products—used as food or as materials. 665-669. Textile Substances of Vegetable or Animal origin. 670-679. Machines, Implements, and processes of manufacture. 680-689. Agricultural Engineering and Administration. 690-699. Tillage and General Management.

A PROGRAMME OF SPECIAL AGRICULTURAL EVENTS

Fruit and Vegetables, Special Display, May 16 to May 24.

Strawberries, Special Display, June 7 to June 15.

Early Grass Butter and Cheese, Special Display, June 13 to June 17.

Trial of Mowing Machines, Tedders, and Hay Rakes, June 15 to June 30. Take Pennsylvania Railroad to Eddington Station.

Early Summer Vegetables, Special Display, June 20 to June 24.

Honey, Special Display, June 20 to June 24.

Raspberries and Blackberries, Special Display, July 3 to July 8.

Trial of Reaping Machines, July 5 to July 15. Take Pennsylvania Railroad to Schenck's Station.

Southern Fruit Products, Special Display, July 18 to July 22.

Melons, Special Display, August 22 to August 26.

Exhibit of Horses, Mules, and Asses, September 1 to September 14. Livestock grounds, Belmont Avenue and Forty-first Street.

Peaches, Special Display, September 4 to September 9.

Northern Fruit Products, Special Display, September 11 to September 16.

Autumn Vegetables, Special Display, September 19 to September 23.

Exhibit of Neat Cattle, September 21 to October 4. Livestock grounds.

Cereals, Special Display, September 25 to September 30.

Potatoes and Feeding Roots, Special Display, October 2 to October 7.

Exhibit of Sheep, Swine, and Goats, October 10 to October 18. Livestock grounds.

Autumn Butter and Cheese, Special Display, October 17 to October 21.

Nuts, Special Display, October 23 to November 1.

Autumn Honey and Wax, Special Display, October 23 to November 1.

Exhibit of Poultry, October 27 to November 6.

AGRICULTURAL HALL

"I sometimes fancied that the Agricultural Hall might reclaim the long-sojourning visitor rather oftener than any other building, if he were of a very patriotic mind. It seems the most exclusively American, and it is absorbingly interesting in traits of its displays." Mr. Howells *was right--the Hall was different--it breathed the atmosphere, the smell and sights of the farm and farm products. The Hall's Gothic gables and huge green roof stood out distinctively in sharp contrast on the fair grounds.*

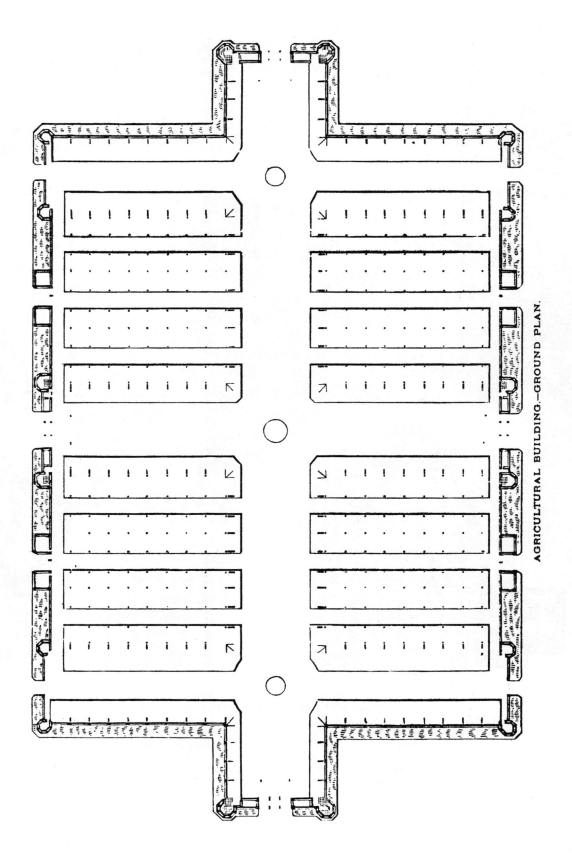

AGRICULTURAL BUILDING.—GROUND PLAN.

**NAVE, LOOKING NORTH. GREAT BRITIAN
AND HER COLONIES, FOODSTUFFS**

*"There were fanciful and effective arrangements;
exhibitions of farm products both foreign and
domestic...literally without number," wrote a
fair-goer. "To remember one was to forget a thousand,
and yet each was worthy to be seen."*

OLD TIME MILL

The mill stood overlooking the exhibits in the central transept of the nave of **Agricultural Hall;** *in turn it was dwarfed by the 75 foot ceiling. An exhibit of operating windmills was found just to the northeast outside the Hall.*

KINGSFORD'S STARCH EXHIBIT

T. Kingsford *and* **Son's** *attractive display was not far from the fountain in the nave. High quality starch was their specialty both for laundry and table use.*

MAIN AVENUE, FOODSTUFFS

The gastronomic delights of the world were displayed along the main aisle--canned and preserved fruits, meats, and vegetables in tantalizing array. A serious and perhaps hungry fair-goer remarked: "We were not restored to our habitual mood of uncritical enjoyment until we came to our favorite case of sugar-cured hams: a glass case in which hung three or four hams, not in the ordinary yellow linen, but in the silk of crimson, white and gold."

HALL NAVE, AGRICULTURAL MACHINERY

Economy and fast assembly had been the main factors to consider when Agricultural Hall was built--wood and glass the materials used. Unfortunately, the roof had developed a leak over the exhibit of mowing and reaping machines--an impressively long aisle of varnished woods and burnished steel. Each Brussel carpeted booth displayed, with pride, a product well made. After a night of rain, the scene was one of desolation as the reaper-men mopped their carpets and carefully dried their machines.

133

Thrifty fairgoers found the three-cent ride on the two-decker steam-driven monorail delightful. It ran between **Agricultural** *and* **Horticultural Halls** *through the picturesque* **Belmont Valley.**

WEST FRONT, OUTDOOR EXHIBITS

Displays too large for **Machinery Hall** *were put outside the west front. "We pass some gas machines of various kinds and iron pipe exhibits, look for a moment at some hoisting machinery, then at pneumatic tubes, busy transmitting messages from one to the other, and stop to examine a gunpowder piledriver, nearby, in active operation."*

The Midsummer Tour

A MIDSUMMER TOUR

A GENERAL SURVEY

By Bayard Taylor

West Philadelphia, Aug. 15.—Coming back, for the first time since the opening on the 10th of May last, to make a general examination of the great Exhibition, I have the advantage of an entirely fresh impression . . . if not all, certainly all important facts and possibilities of our *World's Fair* are finally developed, may be compared and hence invite universal inspection.

It is 9 o'clock, and Monday morning; yet there is already quite a crowd at the gates . . . it takes about ten minutes, we notice; the accomodations for entrance are ample, the stiles turn as if oiled, and the crowd suddenly finds itself in a fair cosmopolitan land, where all sorts of annoyances may look over the high stockade boundary, but cannot enter; where there is order and convenience and rest and refreshment, in addition to what is provided for eye and brain.

The detached buildings, over a hundred in number, are not only finished but set in finished surroundings. There is now no sign of rubbish anywhere; the paths, avenues, and bridges are complete . . . the many full-grown trees scattered throughout the enclosure greatly increase the impression of permanence, and the variety of surface produced by the two dells which, falling toward the *Schuylkill,* divide the blossom-starred plateau of the *Horticultural Building* from the *Main* and *Agricultural Halls,* is now seen to be one of the greatest charms of the spot. The locality is beyond all question the most beautiful which has ever been chosen for an International Exhibition; and the more the disposition of the main and subordinate buildings is studied, the more admirable combination of convenience and picturesque alternation will be appreciated by the visitor . . . Perhaps there are fewer luxurious effects of gardening art— fewer surprises and rapid changes of scene than in Paris in 1867—but on the other hand there is greatly more space and freedom. Considering how much there is, it is amazing that every single feature of the Exhibition is of such easy reach.

The narrow-gauge railway within the grounds is a charming innovation. Let us cross the open, velvet-turfed square between the *Main Hall* and the *Machinery Building,* giving two rapid glances at *Bartholdi's* not-very-successful fountain, and a half a glance with a whole shudder to the fearful and wonderful statue of "Washington Crossing the Delaware" (modeled from Leutze's picture!), and we find ourselves, near the practical and excellent "*Department of Public Comfort,*" at one of the stations of the circular road. We pay five cents apiece and are admitted to the platform. Presently comes up a train of breezy open carriages, drawn by a docile pony locomotive, which makes nothing of grades and short curves. There is no conductor. We take seats among a hundred others, and have scarcely time for another shudder at the marble Washington and an effacing thrill of delight as we pass between the lake, with its great dome-shaped fountain of many sprays, and the level lawn diapered with patterns in geranium and amaranth, when the train halts in front of the *Women's Pavilion.* Here a number of passengers get off although the most of them are apparently bound for the *Government Exhibition* across the way.

In two minutes more we have rounded the head of the dell, looking down upon shady paths none the less fit for lovers, and are in front of the indescribable *Agricultural Building.* This seems to be the chief station on the line. The *American Restaurant* is here, flanked by a beer garden, and *Lauber's* is just across the dell. A little further, there is a building for the display of cheese and butter, while a *Brewers' Hall,* opposite, furnishes the chemical harmony of cheese. The train turns around a small circle in this extreme corner of the grounds, and doubles back nearly to the *Women's Pavilion,* when it darts off down the avenue of *State Buildings,* skirts the whole length of *Machinery Hall,* and returns past *Memorial Hall* (the *Art Exhibition*) to its starting point at the eastern end of the main *Exhibition Building.* The round trip does not take more than fifteen minutes and it is so unique and thoroughly enjoyable that one is tempted to go a second, third or fourth time, for the simple delight of watching the shifting panoramas.

The foreign commissioners, exhibitors, and attendants give a permanent representation of their several nationalities. The native visitors just at present are mostly people from the country, with a sober holiday air about them. It is curious to note their grave, suppressed manner in the morning when they arrive. They stare much and speak little, bestowing their amazement upon great and small things with strict impartiality. The vast extent of the show at first solemnizes them . . . by noon, however, when 20,000 persons are sure to be present, the habits of individual communities grow confused; there is such a vast and variegated crowd that each one returns to his or her natural manner before he or she is aware of it, sure of not being particularly noticed. Then you see strangers giving question and answer or interchanging remarks at every turn. Then the restaurants, the bazaars, and the circular trains are crammed with people who talk freely, laugh and jest at will, and pour out their mixed impressions into the genial common atmosphere. It is not quite the abandon of a European crowd, but a very pleasant approach to it.

I am surprised to find such a small proportion of the better—I should say, the richer—classes of those who live in cities, and claim higher culture and better opportunities of knowledge. It may be that the character of the attendance varies somewhat with the season, and that another month may see a different throng in these wonderful halls; but however it may be, the number of visitors is not half what it should be. The great mass of our people cannot yet understand how much is offered to them . . . it is not so much a holiday show as a great school of instruction . . . two and a half million of paid admissions thus far . . . do not represent more than 800,000 visitors—and there are certainly 4,000,000 persons in the United States who are able to come, and capable of profiting by what they would see.

I should also particularly like to see ten times as many visitors from abroad. The Exhibition will be an incalculable benefit to us in dissipating the notion of our rough semi-civilization which is so prevalent in Europe. The wonder of the foreigner at what is here accomplished is generally mixed with a sense of shame . . . for it is by no means what he anticipated. If Germany, France, and Italy had known much of the country to which they were sending, they would have forwarded their finest instead of their mediocre work, and have spared us many artistic horrors. Great Britain has shown, by her contributions, that she is still nearest and knows us best.

LANSDOWNE VALLEY,
NEAR HORTICULTURAL HALL

A thought concerning the tired and weary had made the **Lansdowne Ravine** *a part of the Exhibition. A visitor described its dells: "Its shady walks, winding in and out between the magnificent forest trees and among the undergrowth; the little babbling brook, as it leaps from stone to stone on its way towards the river, and its secluded and romantic aspect, all unite in inviting the visitor away from the crowds about him, to a contemplative stroll."*

Horticultural Hall

HORTICULTURAL HALL

TOURIST INFORMATION

An allotment of forty acres has been made for the display of tropical plants, and of every variety of garden decoration.

On the north and south sides of *Horticultural Hall* are four hothouses for propagating young plants.

At the west end is located the office of the Department, and a reading room where different horticultural magazines and journals can be found.

A fine view of the interior of the building can be had by ascending the ornamental stairway from the vestibule to the galleries.

Doors lead from the galleries to a promenade around the whole outside of the building. A magnificent view of the entire exhibition grounds and the *Schuylkill River* beyond can be seen from the promenade walkway.

An annex for special displays of flowers is just north of the Hall.

The exhibits in the outdoors department comprise of representative trees of this country, and new plants recently introduced from Japan, China and other parts of the world. Plants and flowers from England, France, Belgium, Germany, the Netherlands, Brazil, Spain, Portugal, and Mexico may be seen in this department. The space reserved for ornamental gardening includes a handsome parterre, or sunken garden, laid off and planted to illustrate the different methods of ornamental flower gardening.

Over three miles of pleasant walks surround *Horticultural Hall.*

HORTICULTURAL HALL

EXHIBITIONS

DEPARTMENT VII.—HORTICULTURE. Classes 700-709. Ornamental Trees, Shrubs, and Flowers. 710-719. Hot-Houses, Conservatories, Graperies, and their Management. 720-729. Garden Tools, Accessories of Gardening, etc. 730-735. Garden Designing, Construction, and Management.

HORTICULTURAL HALL FROM FOUNTAIN AVENUE

Most Americans were fascinated by the Moorish architecture, the slender minaret towers, and the arabesque dome of **Horticultural Hall**. *The promenade balcony on the upper part of the building, with its lovely panoramic view, was an itinerary must to many fair-goers.*

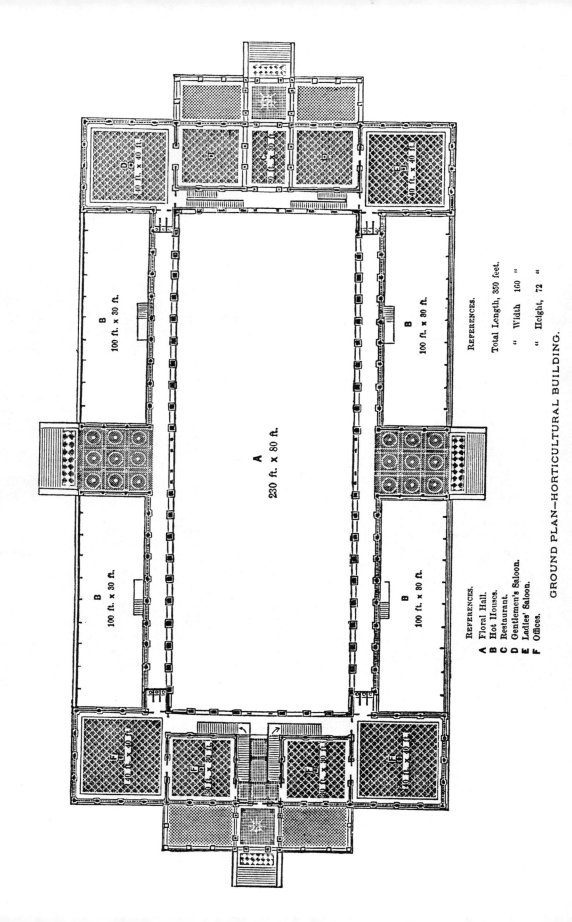

REFERENCES.

A Floral Hall.
B Hot Houses.
C Restaurant.
D Gentlemen's Saloon.
E Ladies' Saloon.
F Offices.

REFERENCES.

Total Length, 350 feet.
  " Width 160 "
  " Height, 72 "

GROUND PLAN—HORTICULTURAL BUILDING.

HORTICULTURE GROUNDS, FROM NORTH BUILDING

Horticultural Hall *was surrounded by grounds covering forty acres, laid out with taste and skill. Displays were beautiful in all seasons. In the spring as the stroller approached north of the Hall, he was treated to a rare and beautiful sight. Inside a framework of canvas were sheltered winding walks with mounds planted in an assortment of English Rododendrons, large and varying in color from deepest purple, crimson, pink, and cherry to pure white. During the warm months the colorful scene was a magnet to home gardeners--"lovely parterres of flowers, exquisite sunken beds in masses of color, clusters of shrubbery and roses, and groups of sub-tropical plants...being laid in a way to equal even European gardens in its beauty and effect."*

HORTICULTURAL HALL FROM EAST GALLERY

The criticisms of the conservatory were many but usually not of a botanical nature. "And if we may hazard a criticism on the interior aspects of the structure, we should say it was unwise to carry vivid polychromatic decoration into the interior of a great plant hall. The colors in columns and arches--due to the many tinted bricks and to blazing tiles--are rich and bewildering and mate fairly well with the Oriental forms of the structure. But, before all, and above all, it is a **Place of Flowers.** *Their coloring is to be considered; and not to be put awry, or cheapened, or subdued, or consumed by the vitreous glare of bricks and tiles." Only* **Miss Margaret Foley's** *beautiful fountain, in the center of the hall, remained above the reach of the critics.*

HORTICULTURAL HALL, MAIN INTERIOR

The conservatory, like a huge hothouse, was redolent of tropical plants and growth. The fireproof basement of the building contained storerooms, heating apparatus, coal-houses, ash pits, etc. It was necessary to control the damp atmosphere and the constant temperature required to keep the exotic plants on display in the best of form.

Annex Buildings

United States
Foreign Nations
State Buildings
Miscellaneous Buildings

UNITED STATES EXHIBITION BUILDING

TOURIST INFORMATION

The most important structure within the enclosure, after the principal *Exhibition Buildings*. It was erected by the United States Government at a cost of $60,000 and covers about two acres. Inside the visitor will find interesting collections and displays of the various departments of the Federal Government and *Smithsonian Institute*. A model Post Office has been set up and supplied with every facility for reception and delivery of mails. Outside a mail car is on display, in complete working order, to illustrate the fast mail service now in operation on our main trunk railroad lines.

FOREIGN NATIONS BUILDINGS

TOURIST INFORMATION

British Commission Buildings—Three buildings located together in a beautiful grove near *George's Hill*. Two are built in sixteenth century style, one resembling the residence of an old English squire. The furniture, floor, tiles, and paper in all are of British manufacture.

The German Empire Building—A handsome brick building. Contains offices of the German Commission, and a reading room where German newspapers may be found. Exhibitors and visitors will find facilities for writing and receiving letters.

The French Government Buildings—The principal building is a pavilion where models, plans, and drawings of the most interesting public works of France are on exhibit. The other pavilions have attractive displays of bronzes, stained glass, church furniture, perfumery, ornamented chairs and setees, garden tents, and much more.

The Spanish Government Buildings—Three buildings. One is a barracks for the Spanish engineers and another—an open pavilion—will be used by them for a summer diningroom. The third building contains various Spanish exhibits of interest.

Swedish Schoolhouse—Erected by workmen from Sweden, and all of the materials used in its construction was imported from that country. Contains schoolrooms and illustrates interior arrangements of Swedish schools.

Japanese Dwelling—Designed to illustrate Japanese architecture and the interior arrangement of their dwellings. Japanese wares will be on exhibition, and for sale, in a bazaar specially erected for the purpose.

STATE BUILDINGS, UNITED STATES

TOURIST INFORMATION

Many of the *State Buildings* are on *State Avenue* adjacent to the *Centennial Fire Patrol* where fire engines are kept in constant readiness, the splendid horses harnessed and attendants on hand to move at a moment's notice.

Registers for recording visitors' names are in each building, and many have newspapers published in the State they represent.

Only a few *State Buildings* have interesting exhibits of local products.

A visitor will note, generally, that *State Buildings* are a rendezvous for hometown or home-state persons.

MISCELLANEOUS BUILDINGS

TOURIST INFORMATION

The Woman's Pavilion.—Handsome structure devoted entirely to the exhibit of woman's work. One quarter of the interior is assigned to foreign countries; handiwork of *Queen Victoria* and her daughters are on display. One third of the building is allocated to womens' works of art; *Mrs. Wormley's* microscopic engravings and wood-carvings are especially worthy of attention. A woman's weekly newspaper, "*The New Century for Women,*" is made up and printed within the building. An annex Kindergarten is nearby where children may be seen in training and study.

Photographic Art Building.—The roof is constructed entirely of glass to insure ample lighting. Erected at a cost of $26,000 from contributions by American photographers. The walls are crowded with photographs from all parts of the civilized world. Some English landscapes are perfectly exquisite, far exceeding the most extravagant hopes of the photographer of fifteen years ago.

The Empire Transportation Company's Building.—Complete exhibition of models, forms, etc. illustrating American system of freight transportation by railroad cars and by steam propelled ships on the Great Lakes. The latest in freight tariffs and information furnished on request.

Shoe and Leather Exhibition Building.—Large building for the display of shoes and leather materials. Machinery in operation illustrating various processes of manufacturing shoes.

Carriage Annex.—Exceedingly handsome display of carriages from many of the prominent builders from all over the world—famous *London* drags, *Philadelphia* phaetons, beautiful carriages from *San Francisco,* sleighs from *Russia,* and luxurious *Pullman* palace-cars. Household appliances and cooking ranges are exhibited in one section of the building.

West Point Cadets' Encampment.—The cadets from the *United States Military Academy* will bivouac on the Exhibition Grounds. The discipline and rules governing their annual encampment will be in force.

DICKSONIA ANTARCTICA, FLORAL HALL

A tree fern from far off **Tasmania.** *A common complaint about Horticultural Hall was that the endless varieties of palms, cactuses, and unattainable bananas soon made the visitor weary.*

FLORAL HALL PASSAGE

"Mounting the marble steps and passing through the vestibule to which they led, the visitor found himself in the main conservatory, a spacious and beautiful hall...The roof was of glass, and the iron framework...decorated in fresco. A light gallery, with railing of open fretwork, extended around it, and opened at each of the four sides of the hall."

UNITED STATES GOVERNMENT BUILDING, SAILING SHIP EXHIBIT

The American visitor could, no matter how infinitesimally small his fiftieth-million share seemed, have a proprietary interest while on government property. The model ships were pronounced very fine by those of nautical bent, as were the many other interesting exhibits. But there was a discordant note about the **United States Government Building**--*"...the open throat of that fearful fog horn, whose blatant notes are the terror of all delicate-eared people for miles around. What the United States, or the officials in charge, can gain by its horrible utterances repeated at all manner of hours, it is hard to conceive. If General Grant has ordered it in resentment of late attacks upon his administration, he is taking a fearful and most unchristian revenge."*

151

UNITED STATES GOVERNMENT BUILDING, TRANSEPT LOOKING SOUTH, NAUTICAL APPARATUS AND SEA CREATURES

Nothing in the Government hall could rival the magnificent display of fish and sea creatures which Professor S.P. Baird, on behalf of the Smithsonian, had put together. There were all manners of fish--stuffed, frozen, and true-to-life photographs of some 400 specimens--all as if they were still in the bower of the sea. However, despite the wonderful display, there were always those who saw things differently, especially on a hot July day--"and in the United States Building we should not have lost patience with the heat if it had not been for the luxurious indifference of that glass full of frozen fishes there, which as they reposed in their comfortable boxes of snow, with their thermometer at 30 degrees, did certainly appeal to some of our most vindictive passions of our nature; and I say during the hot months it will be cruelty to let them remain."

153

JAPANESE BAZAAR

The long low wooden building, covered with corrugated burnt clay tiles of black and white, was built by Japanese workmen and of native materials brought from Japan. "It is said the building was erected at a cost of $15,000...and that it contains goods valued at $90,000, though we think the last estimate is slightly exaggerated." The north front was open with overhanging eaves, and display counters offered many lacquer wares, crockery, bamboo articles, and other handiwork. Inside the building exquisite designs in woodwork and carving adorned the interior and the ceilings, walls, and floors were painted in tile patterns. Outside, the grounds were planted with Japanese flowers and shrubs. The different beds were separated by posts made of bamboo. Lawn vases, urns, and other articles gave a foreign air to the surroundings. Under a bamboo awning were plants sensitive to too much sun. During the construction of the building, it was a source of great amusement to the Americans as to the methods used by the native workmen. Instead of wheeling the American barrows, they carried them as a sedan-chair, back and forth.

BRAZILIAN PAVILION

Just a few months before the **Centennial Exhibition,** **Brazil** *had an exposition in their own country to honor the fiftieth birthday of their emperor,* **Dom Pedro.** *The choicest products of the exposition were sent to the* **Centennial Fair** *for display.* **Dom Pedro,** *who assisted* **President Grant** *in starting the great* **Corliss** *engine on opening day, was greatly admired among the Americans. In addition to the pavilion [above] the Brazilians erected an ornamental court near the north wall in the* **Main Building** *which displayed a wide variety of items including specimens of native birds, maps and drawings, books, coins, jewelry, surgical instruments, wood products, leather, and cottons and canvas.*

PENNSYLVANIA STATE BUILDING

"Wandering on towards the exit-gate, we pass the **Pennsylvania State Building** *facing the lake. Quite a pretenious Gothic structure of two stories, with tower, it contained the usual reception rooms and offices observed in all of these State building."*

ARKANSAS STATE BUILDING

"The next building is that of Arkansas, an appropriate octagonal structure of timber and glass, designed as an exhibition building, and containing a large display of the agricultural and mineral products of the State."

KANSAS STATE EXHIBIT

"Wheat stalks are on exhibition from five to six and a half feet high, with some heads, six inches long, and corn is shown up to seventeen and a half feet high, with ears twelve to fifteen inches in length...there being from seven to thirteeen ears to the stalk. One wing of the building is appropriated to Colorado, whose exhibit is confined exclusively to wild animals and birds native to that State."

MARTHA A. MAXWELL,
HUNTRESS AND TAXIDERMIST

The Colorado Rocky Mountain *exhibit of Mrs.*
Maxwell's *stuffed wild animals proved to be one of the*
Fair's most popular attractions. The bright-eyed little
woman naturalist had hunted and shot the creatures
she displayed. Her pet was a wise old owl, six inches
high, who allowed no one but her to caress him. It was
rumored about that Mrs. Maxwell *was a vegetarian.*

MRS. M.A. MAXWELL IN THE FIELD,
A STUDIO PORTRAIT, 1876

For her achievements as a huntress, her
grateful fellow citizens had presented Mrs.
Maxwell *with a "magnificent rifle, elegantly*
mounted and appropriately inscribed."

KANSAS AND COLORADO BUILDING

KANSAS STATE EXHIBIT

"The interior is quite unique in its decorations. Around the sides are hung sheaves of wheat, rye, and barley; under the dome is a fine bronze fountain from the ladies of Topeka, and above it a full-size model of the Independence Bell, formed entirely of agricultural products of the State."

INDIANA STATE BUILDING

"Adjoining the Ohio building is that of Indiana, which evidently was never favored with the services of an architect in the preparation of its design, the skyline of the gable front being beyond all criticism in ugliness."

MISSOURI STATE BUILDING

The periodic architectural style is brought to reality by the regional architects. It was referred to as "...a small building of no special attraction."

MICHIGAN STATE BUILDING

"...quite handsome in contrast with others, having porches and balconies, and ornamented with scroll work."

NEW YORK STATE BUILDING

"Still farther back, opposite to Delaware, is the New York Building designed in the Italian style, with porticoes and a sloping roof with gables, the whole surmounted by a sort of tower or cupola, and reminding one forcibly of the frame residences so much in vogue several years ago in the neighborhood of the Empire City."

**THE CENTENNIAL. GENERAL VIEW FROM
GEORGE'S HILL SHOWING CAMP OF WEST
POINT CADETS**

*The cadets from the United States Military Academy
followed all the discipline and rules which governed
their annual summer encampments. Beyond the camp,
the open-car train, crowded with sightseers, stands
ready to begin a fifteen minute tour of the grounds. To
the left, foreground, one of the many convenient
turnstile entrances.*

GENERAL WASHINGTON'S CARRIAGE,
CARRIAGE ANNEX

As the story went, **George Washington** *much preferred the back of a horse to the comforts of a carriage. The old general, his memory sacred and hallowed, stood at the apex of the nation's greatness and his relics were well represented at the* **Centennial Exhibition.** *The* **Government Building** *had a display of his camp-bed, table, sword, pistols and clothes. Sharp-witted* **Mr. Howells** *gave the exhibit more than a passing glance--"There are also people of culture...who would sign a petition asking the government to change...the placard on the clothes of the Father of his country which now reads,* '**Coat, Vest, and Pants** *of* **George Washington,'** *whereas it is his honored waistcoat which is meant his buckskin breeches, [pantaloons were then unknown, and "pants" were undreamt-of by a generation which had time to be decent and comely in its speech.] This placard is a real drawback to one's enjoyment of the clothes, which are so familiar, from pictures, that one is startled not to find Washington's face looking out of the coat-collar."*

The Closing Days

THE CLOSING DAYS

The color and warmth of summer quickly passed and as the chill of Fall deepened, the remaining days of the Exhibition were numbered. The judges had been busy flitting from one building to another, testing, making comparisons, and readying their reports. Once their work was complete, the *Centennial Commission* set aside the evening of September 27, to announce the awards.

Judge's Hall was the setting for the long anticipated ceremony amidst a brilliant array of guests. On the stage were gathered the officers of the *Centennial Commission,* the *Board* of *Finance,* the *Board* of *Judges,* the *Foreign Commissioners,* and other dignitaries. A prayer opened the ceremonies, followed by a musical selection given by the *Temple Quartette* of *Boston.* The *Honorable D. J. Morrell, Chairman* of the *Executive Committee* of the *Commission,* gave an address. National airs were then played by the orchestra, after which the *Director-General* of the *Exhibition* made some appropriate remarks in praise of the Exhibition, the exhibitors, and the various commissions. The audience then enjoyed an interlude of vocal music and finally Gen. *Hawley, President* of the *Centennial Commission,* explained the system of awards. In conclusion, he announced that the awards won would be given to the several countries participating, in alphabetical order, thus doing away with any precedence or favoritism of one over the other. The Chief Commissioners of each of the various governments were then to be delivered copies of the awards made to exhibitors from their countries. The *Argentine Confederation* led the list and each representative, in turn, was applauded with enthusiasm as he received his roll of awards. The evening concluded on a musical note.

Exhibitors at the Fair totalled 26,987 and of this number, 8,525 were from the United States. There were 13,148 medals awarded, and 5,134 of these went to the United States.

The great Exhibition drew to a close with regret and sadness, especially because of the forthcoming dismantlement of the many exhibition buildings. *Philadelphia,* it was said, would never be the same. On the evening of November 9, the *Centennial Commission* gave a farewell dinner to the various *Foreign Commissioners* and other distinguished guests—about two hundred and fifty in all. The morning of the 10th dawned with a Federal salute of thirteen guns, which was fired from *George's Hill* by the *Keystone Battery* and simultaneously from the United States steamer *Plymouth* on the *Delaware River.* A slow steady November rain poured down from the gray clouds making the extensive preparations for an open air ceremony out of the question. However, the dismal weather did not keep the crowds away—records showed nearly 122,000 visitors on that day. The scene of temporary seats, one above the other at the west end of the *Main Building* facing the *Bartholdi Fountain* looked forlorn and deserted. The sun would not appear on closing day as it had to herald the opening of the Fair. It was decided that the ceremonies would take place in the *Judge's Hall,* a very small building for the purpose—an unfortunate decision, really, at least for the ladies! To reduce the number of invited guests, admission was refused to those holding ladies' tickets. A few indignant ladies did get past the guards—descendents of important Revolutionary War figures—they said. Seated on a platform, at the upper end of the hall, was *President Grant* and his *Cabinet,* various *Foreign Legations, Centennial Commission, Board* of *Finance,* etc. The *Phildelphia City Troop* acted as *Guard of Honor,* an office performed by them for all presidents since *George Washington.*

The ceremonies opened with *Wagner*'s "*Inauguration March,*" a prayer, a choral and fugue of *Bach*'s, followed by a speech by Mr. *Morrell.* After reviewing the work and struggles of those involved in making the Exhibition a success, *Morrell* directed his attention to future historians, to the great difficulties overcome and hoped for a charitable criticism. At the conclusion of his address, '*Delbingen Te Deum*' was sung by the chorus with effective orchestral accompaniment.

Mr. *Welsh* paid elegant tribute to the memories of the past century. He told of the 8,004,274 paid admissions to the Exhibition (9,910,966 grand total) and of the influence of many nations who had brought with them treasures of knowledge and art. He gratefully acknowledged those home and abroad for their help in the great enterprise.

At the conclusion of Mr. *Welsh*'s speech, the orchestra performed *Beethoven*'s '*Fifth Symphony.*' The Director-General of the Exhibition then delivered an address in which he cordially thanked the foreign commissioners and exhibitors and American exhibitors for their cooperation.

The chorus then sang the '*Hallelujah*' chorus from the "*Messiah,*" after which Gen, *Hawley* delivered an address, reviewing the great difficulties and final success of the Exhibition.

At the conclusion of *Hawley*'s address, the chorus and audience joined in singing, "*America.*" As the song was being sung a stirring flag ceremony took place. The flag, an original one first displayed by Commodore *Paul Jones* on the *Bon Homme Richard,* was unfurled from a window overlooking the platform. Part of the audience cheered while others sang. The flag belonged to Miss *Sarah Smith Stafford* of *Trenton, New Jersey,* daughter of Lieutenant *James Bayard Stafford,* Continental Navy, who had been with *Paul Jones* in the famous engagement with the British frigate *Serapis.*

After the ceremony, Gen. *Hawley* announced that the President of the United States would give a telegraphic signal for stopping the great *Corliss* engine, and at the same moment would announce the close of the Exhibition. President *Grant* then rose, gave the signal with his left hand and said: "I declare the *Centennial International Exhibition of 1876* closed." The announcement came at exactly 3:35 p.m.

The singing of the '*Doxology*' by the chorus and audience ended the ceremony. The President and his suite left the Hall, escorted as they had entered.

In reviewing the great Exhibition, one important result had been the renewal of national acquaintance—the Southerner, the Westerner, and the Northerner had worked together for a giant and grand cause. They had, as they rubbed shoulders, promoted their pride in America and their faith in its future. They had displayed to the world the cotton of Louisiana, the wheat of Kansas, and the mechanical ingenuity of The New England Yankee. The Americans had, as the name United States implied, become once again a united nation.

CENTENNIAL AWARD MEDAL

(Obverse)

The medals awarded by the Centennial Commission were of bronze, four inches in diameter, and the largest of the kind ever struck by the United States Mint. The four female figures on the outside border represent America, Europe, Asia, and Africa. All medals of award were of the same size, weight, material, and design. About 12,000 medals were presented by the Commission.

CENTENNIAL AWARD MEDAL

(Reverse)

PENNSYLVANIA DAY, THURSDAY,
SEPTEMBER 28

The largest day for the Exhibition came on September 28, when 274,919 visitors came to see its wonders. The Pennsylvania State House [above, upper far left] was the center of activity as the delighted politicians mingled with people from the home state. Across the lake, the crowds on Main Avenue wandered by the World's Ticket Office [left foreground] of Cook, Son and Jenkins. The well-informed avoided the Paris Restaurant [facing lake, far right] of the Trois Freres Provencaux--"Not that dishes cooked with so much more sentiment than any you can find elsewhere, but that there are absurd charges for what Americans ordinarily pay nothing for...bread, butter and service...but double and quadruple at the Parisian's place."

THE CORLISS ENGINE, MACHINERY HALL

The giant stationary engine was a symbol of American prestige. On opening day, President Grant's last ceremonial duty had been to start the engine's operation--on closing day his last deed was to shut it off. A strange quiet pervaded the building on exhibition days when the engine was shut off for a noon hour rest. During the interval visitors were entertained by black singers from a Richmond tobacco factory. An impressed visitor wrote of the engine's wonders: "The Corliss engine does not lend itself to description...it rises loftily in the center of the huge structure, an athlete of steel and iron with not a superfluous ounce of metal on it; the mighty walking beams plunge their pistons downward while the enormous fly-wheel revolves with a hoarded power that makes all tremble."

LIST OF PHOTOGRAPHERS

The names of the photographers or publishers appearing here are those whose works are reproduced in this book and listed accordingly. With the exception of two ferrotypes—tintypes—all are taken from a single stereographic photograph, usually of cabinet size.

SELECTED BIBLIOGRAPHY

Arthur's Home Magazine (1875).

Atlantic Monthly (1876).

Authorized Visitors' Guide to the Centennial Exhibition and Philadelphia. Philadelphia: J. B. Lippinoctt & Co. (1876).

A Century After: Picturesque Glimpses of Philadelphia and Pennsylvania. Edward Strahan (ed.). Philadelphia: Allen, Lane & Scott and J. J. Lauderback (1875).

Fine Art of the International Exhibition, The. Strahan, Edward. Philadelphia: Bebbie & Barrie (1875).

Harper's Monthly Magazine (1875); (1876).

Harper's Weekly (1876).

Illustrated History of the Centennial Exhibition. McCabe, James D. Philadelphia: The National Publishing Co. (1876).

Masterpieces of the International Exhibition, The. Wilson, Joseph M. (Illustrated catalogue). Philadelphia: Bebbie & Barrie (1875).

Memorial of the International Exhibition. Burr, Samuel J. Hartford: L. Stebbens (1877).

New York Times (1876).

Quaker Scrapbook. Philadelphia (n.d.).

Record of the Year. Frank Moore (ed.). 2 vols. New York: G. W. Carelton & Co. (1876).

Scribner's Monthly Magazine (1876).

Stranger's Guide in Philadelphia and Its Environs. Philadelphia: Lindsay & Blakiston (1854).

Uniform Trade List Annual. New York: Publisher's Weekly (1876).

United States International Exhibition, The . . . Origin, Rise, and Progress of the Work. Philadelphia: (1875).